3 1257 00700 8489

WITHDRAWN

Schaumburg Township District Library
130 South Roselle Road
Schaumburg, Illinois 60193

What Managers Say,
What Employees Hear

What Managers Say, What Employees Hear

Connecting with Your Front Line
(So They'll Connect with Customers)

EDITED BY REGINA FAZIO MARUCA

PRAEGER

Westport, Connecticut
London

SCHAUMBURG TOWNSHIP DISTRICT LIBRARY
130 SOUTH ROSELLE ROAD
SCHAUMBURG, ILLINOIS 60193

658.45
WHAT

3 1257 01703 8489

Library of Congress Cataloging-in-Publication Data

What managers say, what employees hear : connecting with your front line
  (so they'll connect with customers) / edited by Regina Fazio Maruca.
     p.   cm.
  Includes index.
  ISBN 0–275–98703–5 (alk. paper)
  1. Industrial relations. 2. Business communication.
  3. Customer relations. I. Maruca, Regina Fazio.
  HD6971.W46   2006
  658.4′5—dc22   2005036833

British Library Cataloguing in Publication Data is available.

Copyright © 2006 by Regina Fazio Maruca

All rights reserved. No portion of this book may be
reproduced, by any process or technique, without the
express written consent of the publisher.

Library of Congress Catalog Card Number: 2005036833
ISBN: 0–275–98703–5

First published in 2006

Praeger Publishers, 88 Post Road West, Westport, CT 06881
An imprint of Greenwood Publishing Group, Inc.
www.praeger.com

Printed in the United States of America

The paper used in this book complies with the
Permanent Paper Standard issued by the National
Information Standards Organization (Z39.48–1984).

10   9   8   7   6   5   4   3   2   1

To anyone who has ever served a customer.

Contents

Acknowledgments

My thanks to the following people (and many others, unnamed here) whose support, feedback, front-line stories, and all-around help made this book possible: Barbara Ames, Jane Barrett, Wanda Boeke, Tracie Crowley, Caroline Ellis, Emily Economou, Sean Elliott, Caroline Ellis, Helen and Tony Fazio, Dave Light, Carla Lown, Joan Magretta, Martina Mehl, Audrey and John Peterman and the front-line staff at the J. Peterman Company, June Pye, Kristin Tobin, and Constantine von Hoffman.

My thanks, also, to all of the wonderful people who contributed their thoughts as chapter authors with enthusiasm and a genuine desire to make a difference, to Nick Philipson for his formidable editorial skills and his unwavering encouragement, to the people who worked "behind the scenes" at Greenwood, and to Emily Johnston and the folks at Apex Publishing for the care they took in turning the manuscript into a book.

The inspiration for *What Managers Say* owes a debt of thanks to the research and insights of many professors, consultants, and practitioners, including in particular: Darrell Rigby, a director of Bain & Company, for his 2002 Harvard Business Review article "Avoid the Four Perils of CRM;" Jeffrey Rayport (also a chapter author), for his book *Best Face Forward: Why Companies Must Improve Their Service Interfaces With Customers* (co-authored with Bernard Jaworskki, Harvard Business School Press, January 20, 2005); and Susan Fournier and her co-authors Susan Dobscha and David Glen Mick for their 1998 Harvard Business Review article, "Preventing the Premature Death of Relationship Marketing."

Finally, a very special thank you to Joe, Nina, and Carly for their love, confidence, and patience, and to Joe for saying "why not?" at all the right times.

Introduction

The new chain had taken over the old supermarket about a week before. The store still looked pretty much the same, but there were posters throughout promising great changes, and the employees were all wearing smart new uniforms.

Checking out, I asked the cashier how she liked working for a different company. I recognized her; she had been at that location for at least a few years.

She leaned over the counter toward me and stage-whispered conspiratorially, "You know what? It's terrible here now." She straightened up, looked around her to make sure no one else could hear, and said in a normal voice, "I wouldn't buy the meat here anymore if I were you."

As I drove home, I thought about what she said. When I unpacked the groceries, I poked suspiciously at the package of chicken I'd just bought and then threw it in the trash.

I wondered:

- Was the meat really bad?
- By extension, were the new owners really that bad?
- Would the cashier lie about the meat?
- If so, why?
- If the top managers of the chain had any idea what the front-line employees were saying to the customers, what would they think?

That was when I started taking notes. For the next few months, almost every time I bought something, had a product serviced, browsed in a store anywhere, or placed a phone order, I asked the employees I dealt with a few questions. Did they know anything about the parent company? Did it matter? What did they think of their store, or location, versus the competition? Did they feel the company did right by them, as employees?

Some of them seemed to relish the opportunity to complain, albeit furtively. For example, I heard:

"The people at the top don't care about us. They're just raking it in wherever they are."

"They don't know anything about me, and I don't know anything about them."

Once, when I was looking to buy a children's video from a store that sells and rents them, the employee helping me said, "If I were you, I'd go to [he named another store]. Their prices are much better." When I said, jokingly, "Does the company pay you to say that?" he said, "No, they just don't pay me enough *not* to say it."

Others expressed satisfaction with their immediate surroundings, but also emphasized a gap between them and "The Company."

"I like my job, but it has nothing to do with the people who run the company."

"Corporate sets the rules, but my manager makes sure we're OK. We're not supposed to have water [at the cashier's counter], but he lets us have it anyway because he knows how dry our throats get."

When I asked about how the various organizations made money, I heard:

"We sell more stuff, I guess. That's why this company does O.K. . . . No, I don't think I have anything to do with it."

"I don't know."

"I wouldn't know about that."

"Well, that's the business."

For the record, I also heard many positive comments about parent companies, headquarters, and higher-level (regional) managers. I also encountered several front-line employees who knew a great deal about the levers of profit, margins, the competition, and the company's strategy. (Most of those were salespeople working on commission.)

But to be honest, I was more intrigued by what *didn't* appear to be working, initially, than by what was. (Not unlike rubbernecking when a police car has someone pulled over on the side of the highway. We don't drive around in a state of constant admiration for the superb driving skills of those around us; we don't take notice of them. But when we see someone who has been corralled by the siren and flashing lights, don't we look?)

A few months into this informal research, I started asking people whether they had any advice for the top managers of their companies. Was there something top managers could do to make their jobs at the front line more enjoyable? Could their jobs have more purpose? Could the company do anything to help them better serve their customers? Would it help them to know more about the company's strategy beyond their own locations? In what way?

I heard, among other things:

"The fish rots from the head, if you know what I mean."

"I think it would be good if [top managers] spent more time seeing what we do."

"I don't think there's anything they can do, really. They have to worry about the whole company."

"It would be nice to know how I fit into the picture, but I don't think it would make a difference."

I kept waiting for a silver-bullet response. I kept waiting for one of my interviewees to say something that would make me say, "This is it! This is the word that has to be spread!" But that epiphany didn't materialize.

As time went on, I realized that, for the most part, the front-line employees I talked to could talk very knowledgeably about the dynamics of their immediate surroundings. They could tell me who the "good" workers were among their colleagues; they could tell me about their managers, and sometimes, their managers' managers. They could tell me in a general sense about the company they worked for.

But they had wildly varying ideas on what could make the front-line experience better for them and for their customers. Even those who seemed happy in their jobs and who seemed positioned to offer a top-notch "customer experience" didn't provide the unified, blazing insight I thought I might find.

Reduced to the essentials, the front-line employees I talked to had conflicting thoughts. On one hand, a number of people told me that top managers should get much closer to the front lines. They said senior leaders should spend time regularly doing what front-line employees do, so that they could better understand the customer. The company should be like a family. On the other hand, I heard that top managers *shouldn't* bother to get to know the employees who work at the front lines of their companies. Some people told me that the practice is (or would be) a waste of time. Instead, these people said, senior managers should acknowledge that the two worlds (corporate and point-of-purchase) have little in common and should stop trying to create warm and fuzzy connections where there aren't any to be made.

I also heard that top managers should give front-line employees much more information about the company they work for. I heard that they should make sure that front-line employees are as "in the loop" about strategy, competition, profits, and so forth, as mid- and high-level managers. The front-line people who said this also said that it doesn't matter if the top managers really get to know the front line, per se, but front-line employees should be able to know more about the company for which they work.

By contrast, I heard that top managers *shouldn't* give front-line employees much, if any, information about the company as a whole. Instead, front-line employees should know a lot about the products they're selling and about their local customer base. Information about the organization at large is confusing and often irrelevant.

Faced with this input, I decided it was time to test a few of these themes on a number of very smart people I know who might be interested in the topic. I was confused; I figured someone might be able to set me straight.

I got in touch with Nick Philipson, editor at Praeger/Greenwood. Nick has a great way of turning a good, thorny set of questions into something that might help a few people. The result is this book: a collection of opinions and research-based advice from leading business consultants, academics, and practitioners. Some of the chapter authors have done extensive research on the topic of employee motivation, human resources, and customer experiences. A few are marketing experts, tapped for their understanding of how front-line employees can represent or even personify a brand. Others spend much of their time working with, advising, and/or coaching top managers; and, like all of us, they're also consumers and customers.

CHAPTER GROUND RULES

I left the assignments open-ended. I said that chapters could be relatively short or long. I said that total "opinion pieces" were fine and that case-based chapters were welcome. I encouraged a variety of approaches, ranging from specific advice to top managers on behavior, to suggestions about how front-line jobs might be redesigned or improved, to insights on how the role of the front-line employee has evolved with technology, to thoughts on how evolving strategies have changed (or not) the fundamental role of the front-line employee.

I got what I asked for. And I hope that in these pages, the people who manage front-line employees, the people who manage those managers, and so on will find ideas they can put to good use in their organizations. Every idea presented here is not for every company; the book's intent is not to have readers attempt to stitch together a distended change effort encompassing all of the thoughts herein. But more than a few chapters build on each other's themes, and more than a few float theories or ideas that would complement one another in practice.

Managing front-line employees is a perennial challenge, conducted on a wide range of levels throughout an organization. But a perennial challenge isn't necessarily an unchanging challenge. Nor is it one-dimensional. It is a point-of-contact challenge and a strategic challenge. It requires constant calibration by local mangers and continual monitoring and shaping by those higher up in the organization. It requires new thinking; it also requires revitalized consideration of the tried-and-true. These pages reflect the complexity of the task and the many different levers that can address that complexity.

A MAP OF THE BOOK

The book is divided into four major sections. Part I delves into big-picture issues. How do front-line employees fit into and reflect a company's competitive strategy? What are the essential ingredients of a successful employer/front-line employee relationship? What sparks any given store, or branch, to improve performance, working conditions, and customer experiences in a broad sense? How might top managers rethink what they expect front-line employees to know?

Part II homes in on more specific, behavioral issues. Is it possible to locate the "disconnect" between top managers and the people who serve customers? What common behaviors are more harmful than helpful when it comes to employee training?

Part III offers case-based advice, featuring the experiences of a few companies that have tackled aspects of the front-line management challenge explicitly and with success.

And Part IV takes a step back, literally, and looks to history for inspiration. In the pace of today's marketplace, do we forget or ignore the fundamentals of leadership and motivation?

THE BOTTOM LINE

After I had drafts of all of the chapters in hand, I revisited my pile of interview notes, scribbled on scraps of paper, receipts, and envelopes. I also did several more interviews with front-line employees. Ultimately, I found that there were a few overarching connections to be made from all the different comments and perspectives I'd heard and read. These had less to do with the practicalities of the jobs at hand, or with the strategies conceived or implemented, and much more to do with basic tenets of successful relationships of any type and length: trust, fairness, an appreciation of differences between people and jobs, and the need to belong.

These might look like a laundry list of hokey platitudes in print on a page. (As Rob Galford says, "Beware any managerial advice that can be reduced to 'Do Good; Avoid Evil.'")

But scratch the surface of any of the advice offered in this book, and these fundamental tenets appear for a good reason. People take front-line jobs for a variety of reasons. Some truly enjoy their jobs; others suffer them out of necessity, either temporarily or for the long term. Either way, the lot of the front-line employee isn't easy. Their jobs are often not the first rung on a tall ladder up to better jobs; they're often the first rung of a one- or two-rung ladder. They're generally paid as little as possible. Their jobs, by nature, are often repetitive and boring. They bear the brunt of unhappy customers' tirades but don't often hear when things go right.

Front-line employees clean up, they stock up, they serve, and they come back and do the same thing tomorrow. And even if they're content in their jobs, there's room for improvement—improvement of their own working conditions, and improvement of what they can bring to the company. Increased self-esteem at the front line can result in increased sales. Strengthened trust among store employees and managers can result in strengthened store performance. Reduced angst among front-line employees can result in a better grade of customer service.

Ultimately, top managers' attention to the front-line experience can help create what Ed Lawler calls a "virtuous spiral" that affects customers, employees, and the bottom line, simultaneously ratcheting everything up a notch in quality, performance, and profit.

PART I

Big Picture Essentials

The resort chain's first call center had been in operation for less than half a year. Its managers decided to have the reservation agents try to sell callers a guide to the resorts just after they'd handled their initial requests.

At the end of the first month of this experiment, the managers found the idea to be extremely successful; almost every agent had sold a large number of guidebooks. One agent, however, hadn't sold any.

To try to get a sense of why this agent wasn't performing as the others were, the managers listened in on one of his calls. At the end of the conversation, after he had processed the customer's reservation, he said, "I'm supposed to ask you if you want to buy a guide to the resorts, but they're not really very good. You don't want one, do you?"

The managers quickly met with the agent and asked him to explain. He told them he'd been out sick the day they'd taught the agents how to fill in the form to sell the guide, and instead of asking his supervisor how to do it, he thought it was easier not to sell any.

Did this agent have any idea what the company was trying to gain by selling the resort guidebooks? Did he have any idea how his behavior might be affecting customers' perceptions of the resorts? Did he trust his supervisor enough to confess that he didn't understand a part of his job? Did the supervisor have any idea what this agent had been doing? Did the company provide the kind of environment the agent needed to excel at his job?

It's pretty clear from this anecdote (which I heard from one of the chapter authors in this book) that there were some fundamental elements lacking in the way in which this front-line employee was trained, treated, and tested. Yet the resort is large, well known, and successful. The agent's experience begs the questions: Was his experience an isolated event, or is it indicative of a more widespread problem? What is this business losing at the front line? What is the "opportunity cost" of the way in which its front-line employees are trained, deployed, and managed?

For a "flip-side" perspective, consider this story, told often by management consultant Stefan Sanders in his seminars, about the power of the front line:

There was a time when I was devoted to a particular brand of gasoline. Only that brand of gas could go in our tank. Well one night I was out bowling and bowling and bowling. When I finally noticed the time it was beyond my curfew. (My wife is tougher than I've ever been and I knew the consequences.) As I was blazing a trail back home, the fuel icon started to flash. The more I drove, the faster it flashed. I decided that I had better stop somewhere anywhere and put something in the tank. Put anything in the tank, coffee, peanut oil, soda anything! It just so happened there was a gas station not far from our house, but it sold a different brand.

I pulled into the station and walked up to the pay counter inside. I received a customer service shock. The person behind the counter, working the midnight shift, gave me a heartfelt greeting with a smile on his face. I thought to myself, "What have you been smoking or drinking that is making you this giddy at this time of the night?" I paid for my gas and went outside to pump, all the time keeping an eye out for this strangely happy person! I realized that I paid too much and was due a refund. This meant going back in to see Mr. Happy. The clincher for me was that when he gave me the last bits of my change he said: "Thanks for coming; come back and see us again!"

As I left I was thinking to myself: "This is what I teach. This is amazing. He wasn't being phony!" I decided to return again just to see if this was the only positive person with good customer service. To my surprise I discovered that it didn't matter what time I came in, it didn't matter who was behind the counter; the quality of service was still outstanding. Because of this, I now look for this new brand of gasoline.

It should be noted that the switch was not due to poor customer service by the original company. The switch was produced because one person working a midnight shift alone did it so well that it created brand loyalty. The frontline employee is vital to every organization.

The first six chapters of this book address the big-picture essentials of managing front-line employees. How do front-line employees fit into your strategy? How is your organization set up to serve its customers? What do your customers expect from the people they interact with at the point-of-purchase, or point-of-service? Do your front-line employees have what they need to do their jobs well? How will you know?

CHAPTER 1

Organizing the Front Line: Turning Decisions into Actions

Paul Rogers and Jenny Davis-Peccoud

A telltale sign of any high-performance organization is the engagement and focus of its front line. Those vital employees can build lifelong relationships with customers by delivering the right kind of experience through sales, customer service, and delivery time after time. Employees in the "back room"—the buyers at a retail company, for instance, who decide the next season's assortment of merchandise—are a vital part of the front line, along with cashiers staffing the checkout lines. The best way, indeed the only way, to ensure consistent, high-quality execution is by paying close attention to how the front line is organized.

The same principles that serve customers where the front line is the point of contact apply equally to manufacturers or other industrial companies. Here front-line employees can make or break the quality and cost of the products. For a manufacturer, front-line execution is all about employees on the factory floor boosting their productivity. Whether or not the front line faces the customer, it is a decisive factor in shaping a company's success.

Plenty of companies recognize the importance of the front line but still fall short of delivering consistent, high-quality execution. Often, it's because they haven't turned their front-line strategy into everyday operational reality for the employees who live it. A Bain & Company survey highlights this problem. In a survey of 362 leading companies, nearly 96 percent of respondents recognized the importance of customer focus, and 80 percent believed that they deliver a "superior experience" to the customer. But these beliefs don't survive a simple reality check. When we asked *customers* about the companies they do business with, we found that only 8 percent of companies across seven broad sectors and 47 specific industries actually do deliver a superior experience—superior, that is, in the eyes of the only people who count. Closing this "delivery gap" between the 80 percent of believers and the 8 percent of achievers depends partly on how the front line is organized and led.

What, then, is the hallmark of a high-performance front line? It is their ability to *make good decisions and make them happen.* Front-line staff make critical decisions every day—Should I accept this customer's return? Should I order more components now or next month?—hundreds of thousands of decisions that top management never sees. And front-line employees are ultimately the people who make things happen. They play a vital role in determining the success or failure of strategies devised in the boardroom.

Organizations that excel at front-line execution know how to motivate employees to be passionate and to give their very best, even in positions that involve seemingly uninspiring tasks. High-performing companies manage to foster a connection between the front-line employee and his or her job. It could be that the employee comes from the same target market as a company's customers and understands how to offer extra help that will benefit the customer. It could be that the employee connects with the opportunities afforded by the job at hand. Maybe the employee can see where there is room for self-initiative and opportunity for reward, even within a narrowly defined set of job responsibilities. The result is a virtuous circle. Companies benefit from the energy unleashed by this connection, and employees feel more motivated and fulfilled in their jobs.

In our experience, confirmed through research, there is no silver bullet to foster these connections between employees and their jobs. To create a front line capable of excelling at decision making and execution, the best performers do five things well:

1. *Set a clear vision* that is simple and inspirational to guide people on the front line.
2. *Define clear roles* and hold the people in them accountable.
3. *Hire people with the right skills and attitude,* and focus them on the measures that matter.
4. *Provide the right tools, working practices, and technology* to help people excel at execution.
5. *Instill a high-performance culture* that motivates people at all levels to get things done and to strive for excellence.

Mastering any one of these five areas is admirable in its own right, but it is not sufficient. A company must develop and nurture all five of these elements to help front-line employees realize their full potential.

THE FIVE ELEMENTS IN DETAIL

1. Set a Clear Vision That Is Simple and Inspirational to Guide People on the Front Line

How do you get a front line of thousands of people all working toward a common goal? To accomplish that, a company's leaders need to set a clear vision that is simple and inspiring. The best leaders can express their vision for what it takes to succeed in the business, as well as "the way we do things around here," usually in a single breath. Michael Dell's two-word strategic principle—"Be direct"—sums it up for Dell's 55,000 global employees.

A strong vision must be inspiring; in other words, it must paint a picture of success that motivates employees to become a part of it. Employees need to be able to relate personally to the company's vision to make it effective. ASDA, one of the United Kingdom's leading grocery stores, has a mission to reduce the cost of the average housewife's weekly shop—something that resonates with their employees.

A vision that's too broad can miss the mark. To be effective, a company's vision should contain enough guidance to help employees on the front line make concrete decisions every day about what they should do. American retailer Nordstrom Inc.'s mantra—"Respond to unreasonable customer requests"—empowers employees to take returns from customers when other department stores would reject the request.

A company's vision must be communicated constantly through as many channels as possible. This could include the CEO and top team speaking to front-line employees through broadcasts or newsletters, as they do at ASDA. It might also include top executives rolling up their sleeves and taking shifts on the front line. But a few people at the top can only be in so many places at once. A strong and effective front line depends on leadership that is distributed throughout an organization, within teams at every level of the company. Distributed leadership requires the commitment and initiative of a company's employees, as well as a clear vision about how the business will succeed. As Terry Leahy, CEO of the United Kingdom's leading retail chain, Tesco, said "We don't want one leader. We want thousands."

The power of a common vision is apparent at one U.S.-based restaurant chain. The company launched an impressive turnaround that began with agreement among its senior executives about the right values and priorities—after a clouded vision got in the way of growth. A new strategy championed by one senior executive to move the restaurant to a higher price model had divided the leadership. The plan called for drawing upscale customers with a more innovative menu and higher price points. But same-store sales lagged well behind the industry average, and customer polls showed the plan was not working. Did they have the wrong strategy, or was it poor front-line execution?

In fact, it was both: disagreement and inconsistency at the top about the values and priorities of the business caused inconsistent execution and confusion throughout the company. The vision of the company's restaurant chain as an upscale dining experience was out of step with its history as a casual dining chain offering consistent fare at reasonable prices. Many employees knew it, and so did franchisees, who owned 70 percent of the chain's restaurants.

To get back on track, the leadership team first had to agree that the new strategy wasn't right. The executive backing the drive to move upscale left the company, and the rest of the team took a hard look at how much potential for growth remained in the core business. It turned out to be a lot. The senior executives at the restaurant company decided to rededicate themselves to building the next wave of growth around the company's original values—good food, friendly service, and reasonable prices.

Having agreed to a common vision, however, the company's leaders still had to win the support and enthusiasm of their employees. Here, they had a problem. The dissension at the top of the company had left its mark: the employees had lost confidence in their leaders. At an offsite meeting, the senior team listened to feedback from employee surveys, rating individual and collective leadership styles and the environment they had created. The CEO remembers it as "the worst day in my life."

To earn back the respect of the rest of the organization, the senior executives agreed on four basic ground rules, so they wouldn't revert to their prior dysfunction: build trust, be decisive, be accountable, and hold great meetings. And they defined them practically. For example, building trust meant displaying honesty and integrity, defending team members in their absence, having respect, and eschewing secrets.

If the first step was about developing a cohesive team, the second was to convince employees that they were worth believing in. Once people in the field started to see optimism returning, it became infectious. To help ensure that morale would continue to improve, managers agreed to base a percentage of their compensation on employee feedback.

The company kept the momentum going by hiring people who bought into the new values. Crucially, the restaurant chain also encouraged naysayers to leave through a "no-fault separation" policy, which provided transition pay and assistance in finding a new job. With clear leadership and the new direction, employee turnover subsided. Same-store sales growth went from 0 to 4 percent—well above the industry average. The stock price has increased more than fourfold since 1999.

Setting a clear vision is the first step in creating a high performance front line. Make it clear and simple, communicate it often, and ensure that everyone—from the board room to the front line—acts in a way that brings this vision to life.

2. Define Clear Roles and Hold the People in Them Accountable

To be effective, people need to know what they are expected to do, and they need to feel accountable for doing it. This is just as true on the front line as it is for the executive team. When people are unclear about their roles, decision making suffers; when roles are clearly defined, it paves the way for decisions to be made quickly and consistently.

Defining roles for the front line means being clear about the scope of the job you are asking people to do. Sometimes this means pushing decision-making authority out to the front line. Other times it means clarifying that a given role is restricted to execution, with little decision authority. Despite the volumes written on "empowerment," there is no single right answer for defining front-line roles. Companies must think through what is right for a given situation with a given set of employees. It is just as important to clarify what a group of employees is *not* responsible for as it is to outline which decisions and responsibilities lie within their remit.

In addition to clarifying roles, companies need to structure the front line so that employees can perform effectively in the roles assigned to them. The key is identifying what we call "linchpin" employees. These are usually front-line supervisors, at some level, who provide coaching, direction, and guidance to front-line teams. In a department store, for example, the linchpin employee is not the store manager but the manager of a particular department. For a manufacturing company it might be the shift supervisor. By structuring these jobs with the right number of direct reports and giving the linchpin employee the specific role of developing the front line, these employees can have a huge impact on front-line effectiveness.

One company that has excelled at defining the role of their front line is Timpson, a leader in shoe repairs and key-cutting in the United Kingdom. During the last 10 years, Timpson's revenues have increased fivefold and its profit has tripled. Employees' average earnings per week, unadjusted for inflation, have increased 53 percent. In 2004, Timpson ranked No. 2 in the 50 Best Workplaces in the United Kingdom.

A large part of Timpson's success results from the clearly defined roles of its front-line staff. Says Chairman, CEO, and owner John Timpson: "The people who serve our customers run the business, everyone else is there to help." John Timpson has given everyone on the front line the authority to make decisions. For example, the Timpson price list is a "guide," with front-line employees empowered to set their prices where they want and give discounts if they feel it is warranted by the situation. Store managers order their own stock from Timpson warehouses, not relying on a centralized electronic system to do it for them. Every front-line employee has the authority to spend up to £500 to settle a complaint.

As a result, Timpson's front-line employees are clear about their role and feel accountable to deliver. They have simple guidance from the top—"amaze our customers"—and they know the bounds within which they can operate to achieve that goal. Their incentive to use authority wisely is reinforced by the share they receive in the success of the business: the more they sell, the more they earn, with no limit, through Timpson's weekly bonus scheme.

Timpson has also recognized the importance of linchpin employees. Area managers are encouraged to spend as much time as possible in the stores. A key task is building their teams' skills, along with the business. Branch managers also are linchpin employees, responsible at the store level for driving results. Timpson recognizes linchpin employees at several levels in the organization, so the company created wide salary bands to motivate people at every level to do their best. A high-performing branch manager can earn more than an area district manager and possibly more than an area manager.

Anyone who is unclear about the role of the front line at Timpson need only look at the sign in every shop, which states, "The staff in this shop have my total authority to do what they think will best give our customers an amazing service." Or they could just look at the results, which show strong revenue and profit growth, as well as a resounding vote of confidence by employees that Timpson is where they want to work.

Defining clear roles for front-line employees is the next step in unleashing the full potential of the front line. Be clear about what each person is, and isn't, responsible for. Ensure that these roles are broadly understood throughout the organization. And follow through with coaching from linchpin employees to help front-line employees develop and give their best.

3. Hire People with the Right Skills and Attitude, and Focus Them on the measures That Matter

Getting the right people and ensuring they are all pulling in the same direction are critical to ensuring front-line success. Doing so depends partly on the right recruiting strategy and people development processes. The rest comes down to a company's measures and incentives for its front-line staff. Neither is easy. Some front-line jobs are low-skill and low-pay. Turnover is a perennial problem. Increasingly, companies are outsourcing some activities that used to be performed by a company's own front line. High-performance organizations manage to address these challenges creatively.

Because the front line is the everyday expression of a company's values and proposition, the type of people a company deploys on the front line can act to reinforce, or undermine, customers' perceptions of the company. Front-line leaders often hire for attitude as much as for skills. Timpson is a case in point. The company used to recruit for shoe polishers and key cutters. However, John Timpson realized that not all of the "experts" came with the attitude required to amaze their customers. He scrapped the company's traditional recruiting process and instead told his recruiters to "Hire personalities." He designed a sheet of cartoon characters and told recruiters to tick whether a candidate seemed to be a "Mr. Ambitious" and "Mr. Friendly" or a "Mr. Scruffy" or "Mr. Dishonest." Using this simple tool, Timpson recruiters began to build a front line that was outgoing and committed to success.

ASDA, like its parent Wal-Mart Stores Inc., has also targeted its recruiting efforts, focusing on people who by nature are more gregarious and therefore more likely to enjoy interacting with customers. ASDA executives talk about "auditioning" rather than "interviewing." Many who pass ASDA's "audition" are more than 50 years old. Called "Goldies" because they've celebrated their golden or 50th birthday, ASDA believes that older employees are more likely to deliver the type of customer service in store that the company is looking for, in part because they match the demographic profile, interests, and usually the values of ASDA's core customers.

In addition to getting the right people into the business, front-line leaders also ensure that those people are focused on the measures that matter and are paid in a way that reinforces the behaviors they are looking for. One of the keys here is to ensure a balance between productivity and customer service. eBay is a great example of a company that understands this point.

At eBay, customer feedback is weighted alongside productivity in creating employee performance reviews. eBay collects input through continual surveys and monthly two-day workshops with buyers and sellers to ensure that customers' needs inspire and drive any department or business unit's efforts to boost productivity.

eBay is not alone in using measures and incentives to motivate the front line to deliver outstanding performance. Ireland's Superquinn supermarket chain rewards employees based on customers' behavior. For example, the bakery staff in one store rose to a challenge to increase the number of households that purchase from the bakery. The prize was a helicopter trip around the local area. The team decided to offer people coming into the store a free doughnut tasting and guaranteed every doughnut sold would be less than 15 minutes old. The result: households purchasing from the bakery hit 90 percent, up from 75 percent (measured by loyalty card data) and the entire team won helicopter trips.

Getting the right people into the business and focusing them with measures and incentives tied to success are other traits of companies with outstanding front lines. Look for attitude as well as skill. Let your measures, more than just your words, convey what you want the front line to focus on. And get creative with incentives. It's not always about money—sometimes companies with the best front lines pay significantly less than their competitive counterparts. But they find other rewards that motivate their people.

4. Provide the Right Tools, Working Practices and Technology to Help People Excel at Execution

You can't build a house without a hammer, and you can't deliver outstanding front-line performance without the right tools and techniques. Whether it's providing great in-store service for a retailer or driving highly efficient extraction or production for a diamond company or steel mill, arming the front line with the tools to do the job is a hallmark of the best performers.

ASDA's success was built partly on its attention to giving its front line the tools and practices to excel. After a move into higher-end supermarkets stalled, ASDA's leaders refocused the company on its core business: delivering value through everyday low prices and a deep commitment to local customer needs. The new management team set the company's sights on rebuilding ASDA's market position as a low-price leader. They realized that outstanding front-line performance and commitment would be critical to the turnaround.

In the early days of the turnaround, the leadership team dedicated significant time to communicating the new vision of the company to all of ASDA's employees. But ASDA went further than just communicating the importance of the customer. It armed its front line to deliver. For example, it set up a data room to collect best demonstrated practices from around the system, documenting and coordinating the most effective approaches in stores. Out of this the "ASDA Best" hallmark was born, in which good ideas in a particular store are reapplied and celebrated across the whole network. Stores were encouraged to innovate new ways to motivate the front line, resulting in literally hundreds of new ideas. One example is the "golden trolley," a piece of backroom equipment painted gold and reserved for the use each week by the warehouse employee whose commitment to ASDA has been singled out.

To ensure that the front line knows how to apply these tools, ASDA made a critical decision to make their store managers accountable for one overriding task, managing the people working in the store. Unlike many other retailers, where store managers attend to every aspect of operations, from the front door to the loading dock, ASDA's managers focus on helping the front-line employees master the tools and techniques that make ASDA a great customer experience.

The results have been impressive: ASDA moved from the brink of bankruptcy in the early 1990s to one of the best-performing companies in the U.K. retail sector. ASDA today is one of the United Kingdom's largest retailers, with 265 stores and 135,000 employees, of which many are part-time. Its market position as a provider of "everyday low prices" and its strong performance culture attracted the interest of another leader in frontline execution—Wal-Mart, which acquired ASDA in 1999. The acquisition was a validation of ASDA's operational excellence and strategy, particularly as Wal-Mart was eager to learn some things about front-line execution from its new U.K. business. Indeed, ASDA's response to a challenging retail environment in the United Kingdom has been to reduce the number of middle managers by 1,400 in order to hire more front-line staff.

Giving the front line the right tools is a must-have, not a nice-to-have. Look for the best across the system. Get the tools into the hands of the people who need them. Don't underestimate the power of the "linchpin employees" on the front line to put tools to work in the most effective ways.

5. Instill a High-Performance Culture That Motivates People at All Levels to Get Things Done and to Strive for Excellence

Plenty of companies have "fun" or "vibrant" cultures, but relatively few manage to make their business objectives and their overall vision live and breathe through the thousands of employees on their front line. Great companies foster a passion for the business that encourages people to give their best and at the same time create a more fulfilling workplace for the employee.

Every company's culture is different, of course. But companies that achieve this level of commitment have a common characteristic—an internal compass that guides employees to act according to the company's values, even when no one is watching. Companies with high-performance culture inspire loyalty from employees, who want to stay and be part of a team. They create advocates, who are positive about the business to customers, colleagues, and recruits. They find ways to give meaning to jobs, particularly on the front line, so that employees feel that work is worth their energy and commitment. Leaders on this dimension are 31 percent more likely than the average company to have a culture focused on performance. They don't take culture for granted; they manage it. That's a tall order because it requires engaging people's inherent beliefs about the value they place on their work and contributing to a common enterprise.

Enterprise Rent-A-Car knows the value of a strong culture. The largest car-rental agency in the United States—it passed Hertz for the #1 ranking in 1996—Enterprise leads the market for neighborhood and off-airport rental cars, where people rent because they need a replacement vehicle while theirs is in the shop for repairs or because they want to take a short business or leisure trip. Enterprise built its industry leadership, in large part, by establishing a culture that connects performance with customer loyalty and instills the conviction among employees that attention to customers' needs leads to success.

"Put customers and employees first, and profit will take care of itself," declared founder Jack Taylor, and Enterprise leaders ever since have taught that philosophy to managers and employees throughout the organization. CEO Andy Taylor and President Don Ross make a point of addressing training classes of new managers on Saturday mornings. They relate examples of outstanding customer service to reinforce their message, like the story of one branch employee who accompanied the wife of a customer stricken by a heart attack to the hospital and stayed with her for hours until relatives arrived.

On a day-to-day basis every employee in every branch is focused on the "Enterprise Service Quality index" (ESQi), which measures how satisfied customers were with their rental on a five-point scale. Rental branches' score on that metric is the key variable in determining promotions for branch managers and employees. So everyone learns that he or she must take personal responsibility for turning customers into enthusiastic promoters of Enterprise. As the company explains, ESQi is "one of many ways in which we remind ourselves to put customer needs first."

Cultures such as Enterprise's truly emerge in a crisis, when employees must think and act quickly without guidance from headquarters. Enterprise faced a dilemma in the aftermath of September 11, 2001, as stranded travelers desperately sought cars to return to their homes. Enterprise ordinarily doesn't rent one way; its neighborhood branch system lacks the logistics and operations to track and offer one-way rentals. But many branch managers quickly decided to give customers the cars anyway and worry about how they would get them back later on.

The response came as no surprise to Enterprise employees. One sign of a strong, effective culture is that everyone in the company understands what to do without being told. Three days later, with the nation's transportation system still crippled, Enterprise headquarters issued a policy instructing branches to permit out-of-state one-way rentals for stranded travelers and to waive or reimburse drop-off fees. "There will be losses," said CEO Taylor, who stayed in touch with employees via e-mail during the crisis. "But right now we're just concerned about taking care of our customers." His managers, as it happened, were out ahead of him.

Enterprise's cultural cornerstone of "Put customers and employees first, and profit will take care of itself" has certainly proved true. Privately held, the company doesn't report its profits, but the firm's worldwide revenues have grown 32 percent between 2000 and 2004, to $7.4 billion, helping to establish Enterprise as the leading car rental company in North America.

Building a high-performance culture among front-line staff may be the most challenging element of outstanding front-line performance. Yet, it is also perhaps the most critical. Know what you stand for. Manage the culture to match. And support employees who act to reinforce the culture.

PUTTING THE BEST FOOT FORWARD

Building a high-performance front line requires companies to do five things well: set a compelling vision, define clear roles, hire the right people, provide strong tools, and build a high-performance culture. It takes a system, not just a structure. For a company faced with the need to turn around a front line that is underperforming, or for one hoping to turn an adequate front line into a true source of high performance, the task of building such a system may seem daunting.

The first step is to identify where to start. A quick diagnostic of what works well and what needs to be improved can often point to one major issue that needs to be tackled first. It is critical not to underestimate the change process. It may be possible to analytically determine the right front-line structure or the appropriate balance between productivity and service in employee metrics, but it is impossible to turn those into reality without winning the hearts and minds of thousands of individuals. The change process is almost as critical as making the right changes.

These investments pay off enormously for employers as well as front-line employees in the short term and over the long-term. Companies that succeed in building a strong front line find that it becomes an enduring source of competitive advantage. When people on the front line give their time and energy to making the business succeed, competitors have a hard time keeping up.

CHAPTER 2

How Should the Front Line Really Treat Your Customers?

Paul F. Nunes and Woodruff W. Driggs

Front-line employees have become victims of overheated management rhetoric about customers. Gurus and executives alike wax lyrical about the need for companies to get "close to their customers" so that they can achieve something called "customer intimacy." The pressure is on front-line employees (at point-of-sale locations, call centers, billing departments, and so forth) to deliver. But the goals do not discriminate; "the customer comes first" is a near-universal mantra, regardless of the product, service, or company in question. Certainly no company wants to discourage its employees from providing good customer service whenever possible. The problem is that many companies lack clarity about what they hope to gain from their efforts in this regard.

As a result, some companies inadvertently send mixed and incorrect signals to their employees, demanding efficiency in their customer interactions, but also simultaneously expecting them to go the extra mile.

Other companies go to the opposite extreme, squandering large amounts of hard-earned resources or profits on initiatives while expecting better profit margins. That myopia can literally turn customers into a waste of time. It can also run a company into the ground, leading not so much to unhappy or confused employees as to no employees. For example, the now-defunct Internet grocer Streamline at one point gave out $50 credits to customers who experienced late deliveries, even to people who were already extremely loyal and unlikely to cancel the service over one mistake. This is not an isolated example. In certain industries, large investments designed to achieve high levels of customer satisfaction cannot guarantee a return in the form of greater loyalty. When a hot new automotive product is introduced—for instance, the PT Cruiser, the Mini Cooper, or the Hummer, people in the market for a trendy vehicle won't hesitate to abandon the brand they've owned in the past. But many companies continue to over-deliver in their efforts to win loyalty either because they can't or won't calculate the real impact that customer-satisfaction initiatives have on their business performance.

Customer satisfaction, then, is not necessarily the be all and end all of good business. It's no substitute for a solid business model or a well-thought-out and carefully executed strategy. And there's the rub: whereas most companies develop an overall strategy in response to industry dynamics after an analysis of their own distinctive capabilities, they fre-quently neglect to create a strategy that can serve as a guide for interac-tions with customers. Yet in today's marketplace, with its dizzying array of products, variations, and point-of-purchase options, such a strategy is becoming increasingly necessary. Every company needs a strategy, devel-oped in concert with its competitive strategy, that clearly expresses how it intends to treat customers. That is, companies need a customer interaction strategy that specifies the level and quality of the relationships and the degree of differentiation from competitors' approaches based on a larger strategic view of how they plan to compete.

Only with such a strategy in place can a company be sure that it is using its resources—including its front-line employees—wisely.

HOW A CUSTOMER INTERACTION STRATEGY GROWS OUT OF A CORE STRATEGY

How should managers think about planning and implementing a cus-tomer interaction strategy? It helps to begin by considering the three core or "generic" strategies introduced by strategy scholar Michael Porter in 1985: cost leadership, differentiation, and focus (or niche). These catego-ries can be applied fruitfully to the problem of crafting a customer interac-tion strategy as well. But the solution can't automatically be one in which the company's generic strategy is identical to its customer interaction approach. In some instances, the two should line up directly, but in oth-ers, a company's "back" (generic or overall) strategy should be different from its "front" (customer interaction) strategy. (Table 2.1 shows the nine possible permutations of this front-back framework.) In fact, some suc-cessful companies have developed front-back hybrids that have helped them find unique positions within their industries.

Composite Strategies

It may seem that all successful companies are extremely dedicated to their customers, but they don't all lavish the same level of service on

Table 2.1
Composite Strategy

		Customer Interaction Strategy (Front Strategy)		
		Cost	*Differentiation*	*Niche*
Generic Strategy (Back Strategy)	*Cost*	**Low, Low Cost** Minimize expense largely by replacing people with technology	**Compensation** Spend a little extra to counter-balance low-cost strategy effects	**Angel Customers** Invest to better identify and serve the most profitable segments
	Differentiation	**First Do No Harm** Achieve high-volume, low-cost sales without dam-aging brand value	**Distinct Differentiation** Create a differentiated customer experience to complete the overall unique experience	**True Loyalty** Build relation-ships with those that value your differences
	Niche	**Profitable Niches** Use technol-ogy-enabled efficiency to create more profitable and additional niches	**Defend and Extend** Add differenti-ated service to prevent entry and thwart rivals	**Extreme Focus** Invest to better identify, relate to and serve target customers

Source: Accenture Analysis.

them. Rather, their front-back approach as a whole dictates how they treat them. An exploration of each hybrid shows how the three front strategies uniquely support the three traditional generic or back strate-gies. Managers who understand the benefits of these nine approaches can begin to line up their messages to employees so that their actions come to speak as loudly as their words.

COST-LEADERSHIP FRONT STRATEGIES

The fundamental purpose of a low-cost customer interaction or "front" strategy is to create or preserve the profitability of the core or "back" strategy. In general, a low-cost customer strategy works best when the core strategy is demonstrably successful. When it comes to customers, companies that follow this approach *do* spare expense, and wisely so.

In a *low, low cost* combination, the back and front strategies are aligned. Companies that take this approach leverage a low-cost interaction strategy to maintain their overall low-cost strategy and position. Few companies will openly admit to sharply limiting their investment on customer service, but many follow this practice, especially industries populated by low-cost competitors. The near absence of sales staff at any number of big-box and deep-discount retailers is an example of this reality, and it is easy to understand its necessity if the business model is to succeed. Those businesses occupy a position in which a few customers will leave because of bad service, but many customers will leave if prices go up.

Low-cost airlines are another example of businesses in which the front and back strategies line up nicely. Companies such as AirTran, ATA, JetBlue, and Midwest have all outperformed their larger hub-and-spoke counterparts by a wide margin. These airlines offer their customers a no-frills experience as a way of saving costs, some of which they pass back to travelers. European low-cost carrier Ryanair, for example, chooses not to sell snacks during flights because they make the aircraft more difficult to clean, which increases the servicing time and reduces an aircraft's rate of utilization. The airline also chooses not to have reserved seating because it believes that passengers are better about showing up on time when a potentially better seat is at stake. These low-cost customer interaction approaches are well aligned with the elements of a low-cost back strategy, such as flying only one type of aircraft in order to reduce maintenance costs.

Companies with a *first do no harm* strategy, on the other hand, combine a back strategy based on significant differentiation with a front strategy that recognizes the need to control customer interaction costs. Companies that lead the way on product innovation are likely to benefit from this strategy. Mass-market carmakers with hot-selling new vehicles, for example, can justify limiting their investments in dealership amenities for a time: why go overboard spending on customer service when there is high demand and no substitutes exist? In such cases, loyalty is not at stake; smart companies know that there is almost no such thing as loyalty in certain markets, in particular those that are driven by fashion or a fast pace of innovation, such as clothing and consumer electronics in addition to automobiles. Companies in these industries do not ignore customers—far from it. But they do not seek advantage or even parity with competitors through customer interactions if investments in those interactions cannot be traced to a better bottom line. Like doctors with their patients, the first rule they follow with their customers is "do no harm."

The field of healthcare in general has taken this approach. Most HMOs are so focused on "sweating the assets" (quite literally, as some HMO doctors handle as many as 3,000 patients) that they spend as little as they can get away with on customer interactions. (Spurred by competition, some traditional healthcare providers have reconsidered their neglect of customer interactions. For example, the emergency department of University Hospital in Augusta, Georgia, conducted a so-called experience audit of its patients and their families in the late 1990s and used the results to justify a broad range of changes that made trips to the emergency room easier to bear.[1])

The final low-cost front strategy blends with a niche back strategy to create *profitable niches*. In this scenario, companies use a low-cost structure in customer sales and service to make selling to a limited customer base more profitable, and in many cases, such as the many Internet-based companies, profitable at all. Netflix is a good example of this strategy in action. The company targeted video renters who find returning videos on time inconvenient, as well as those who find traditional rental store selections too limiting (Netflix offers 55,000 titles, including nearly every feature movie available on DVD). The company paired a mail-order business model with a low-cost Web-based front end to grow quickly and occupy an attractive niche. The company delivers many extra benefits to customers through its Web-based system, including movie recommendations based on a customer's rental history, but the overall business model's success still relies on a front strategy of low-cost customer interactions.

The low-cost front strategy is also helping niche businesses that existed before the Internet age. Successful gourmet food retailers such as Omaha Steaks and Harry and David, among others, have been able to increase sales to a select set of customers through low-cost online customer interactions. The Internet is a two-edged sword, however, as it also allows new rivals to enter a market relatively easily. Any niche company's back strategy must be robust enough to withstand these challenges, regardless of its low-cost front strategy.

DIFFERENTIATED FRONT STRATEGIES

A differentiated front strategy is best and most often used to strengthen the value proposition of the back strategy through the creation of another level of distinction in the marketplace. Differentiation is often a critical front strategy when the back strategy is under attack from competitors or is in transition as the business environment evolves. Yet it can also serve to put extra distance between companies leading the pack and their competition.

Compensation, for example, involves using little extras in the way of customer service to counteract the naturally unlikable parts of a low-cost back strategy. Wal-Mart's greeters and Southwest's fun-loving and often zany cabin crews are just two examples. Those companies are using relatively minor investments to achieve a disproportionate and differentiated effect on customer satisfaction while still maintaining their low-cost leadership. It makes even more sense for these companies to take this approach because of the market-dominant cost position they each enjoy. Similarly, Home Depot and Lowe's, the do-it-yourself giants, offer a stream of clinics and workshops to their customers, as well as design services. These investments, however, are more than just extras; they are direct stimulants of increased sales.

The compensation strategy is not without risks, of course. Amazon.com's stock fell in the first quarter of 2005 at least in part because of investments by the company aimed at differentiating its Web site from that of competitors. Such short-term gambles are a necessary part of any strategy, however, and Amazon's focus on compensating for a low-cost back strategy with differentiated customer interactions may bear fruit over the long haul.[2]

Companies that seek *distinct differentiation*, meanwhile, use their customer interaction strategy to reinforce the core ways they are different from competitors. BMW, for example, already positions itself as the manufacturer of "the ultimate driving machine." But it also seeks to be different on the front end. For example, the company surveys its customers after every dealer service visit, and only the highest rating across the board counts toward a dealer's target goals with the manufacturer. This prompts dealers to check with their customers multiple times to determine whether they are receiving not just good, but outstanding service.

Even this degree of attention to customers may not be enough to impress buyers of luxury cars, however, who have a wide variety of options to choose from today. In this segment of the market, investment in dealership amenities may be the wise course to follow. The Nalley Automotive Group, for example, is investing heavily in its Atlanta-area dealerships. One of its Lexus dealerships, built at a cost of $20 million, features a Starbucks coffee bar, a clothing boutique, and a lounge with wireless Internet access; a nearby BMW dealer includes a pet area complete with dog treats.[3]

Such spending can spiral out of control, of course, and can be copied by those willing to spend the money. It's not a good bet for mass-market dealers. Still, differentiation with customer interactions is not just a luxury-car approach; it has been a winner with Saturn, too. Whatever the market or industry, companies that combine differentiated products and services with differentiated customer interactions produce unique experiences for their customers. In the medical field, concierge medical practices such as MDVIP, where customers can pay $1,500 a year to sign up with a doctor who treats only 300 patients, are now gaining popularity.

Finally, focused companies with a differentiated front strategy *defend and extend* their niche position; they defend it from imitators and extend it to capture other niche positions as well. Harrah's Entertainment, for example, has spent heavily to keep customers whose primary focus is gambling rather than shopping or seeing a show. A good part of the company's recent success has resulted from innovative use of technology; it is able to mine data, for example, to contact customers by phone or mail who have spent a lot of money at Harrah's but not in the recent past. The company also used its large trove of data to design a three-tiered loyalty-card program in which the benefits of being in the highest or middle-tier are so clear that customers are inspired to spend more to move up a rung.

But technology is only part of the story. The gaming juggernaut also trains its employees to be masters of customer service. To help everyone from slot attendants to housekeepers learn how to deliver service that is both fast and friendly, Harrah's puts all employees through a certification program. At every Harrah's location, financial incentives are tied to improved customer satisfaction ratings for the facility as a whole; thus a team-first attitude is encouraged and weak links bring everyone down. And higher revenue takes a back seat to happy customers, at least for these purposes: outstanding financial results at a location combined with mediocre customer satisfaction scores mean no bonus. In just a couple of years, however, Harrah's had paid out tens of millions of dollars in bonuses to its employees. This differentiated customer interaction strategy is paying off in strong revenue gains even in down markets.[4]

FOCUSED FRONT STRATEGIES

A focused or niche customer strategy always concentrates on capturing an opportunity when paired with one of the three back strategies. Yet it strengthens each in a different way, either by targeting a subsegment of high-profit customers, focusing on a much larger but still unique segment of the mass market, or going after all customers but treating them as segments of one.

When paired with a low-cost back strategy, a focused front strategy concentrates on *angel customers*. Companies following this composite strategy seek to serve the mass market while at the same time offering better service to the most profitable customers (and charging for it where possible). Although focusing on highly profitable customers may always seem like a good idea, such a strategy makes particular sense when there are advantages to having a large-scale operation—such as those found in the retail, entertainment, or process industries—and yet profitability among customers varies dramatically.

This is the case, for example, in the consumer electronics industry. BestBuy reaches its angel customers through six research-identified segments. It has modified its stores, its processes, and its product and service offerings to better capture the opportunity these segments represent. At the same time, less-profitable customers can also shop at its stores and find what they are looking for at competitive prices.

BestBuy has recently opened concept stores in the Chicago area called Studio D and Escape. In its design, Studio D resembles a women's boutique, and Escape has a hip, urban look meant to attract high-tech mavens. Each store is less than one-tenth the size of a typical BestBuy big box, and each seeks to draw customers who might spend hours learning how to make a digital scrapbook, print large-format photos, or learn about the latest cell phones with their burgeoning functionality. In addition to providing classes for groups within the stores, Studio D sends people to schools and community events to demonstrate how to use digital cameras. At Escape, people can get a membership for a small fee that will allow them, for example, to rent a video game console with the latest video games in one of four themed "pods" or rent a "luxury box"—a partitioned area that can hold up to 10 people who can then enjoy watching a large-screen plasma television on comfortable furniture while eating catered food. While experimental, these new stores may help BestBuy to maintain a fundamentally low-cost strategy that is modified by a niche customer-interaction strategy in carefully targeted markets.[5]

When companies combine a differentiation back strategy with a focused front strategy, they are seeking *true loyalty*. These businesses use focused customer interactions to ensure that their differentiated offerings are efficiently and effectively delivered to customers who truly appreciate them. Thus loyalty, not just profitability, is the test. The strategy relies on clarifying an offering's distinctive proposition in the customer's mind (and often in the company's mind) and establishing a bond with those who find the proposition uniquely attractive. The offerings, however, remain largely mainstream or mass market.

Apple Computer, for example, has fanatically devoted customers who love its products, differentiated both by their design and their functionality. The company reaches its expanding customer base through hip urban stores, a Web site that sells physical products and virtual ones (iTunes), and ad campaigns that stress the uniqueness of the company and, by implication, the customer (Think Different). In fact, advertising campaigns can be thought of as part of a customer interaction strategy that leads to true loyalty. That's one of the reasons Mountain Dew has become the third most popular soda in the world, behind Coca-Cola and Pepsi. Its ads have captured the attention of young people who see themselves as outside the mainstream.[6]

The third variation on a niche front strategy concerns companies that achieve an *extreme focus* by combining focused customer interactions with a niche back strategy. Companies with this composite strategy acquire deep knowledge of existing and target customers and then spend what it takes to be desirable and attractive to them. For example, most luxury hotels seek to maintain a niche by reinforcing their value proposition to their wealthy clientele in all that they do.

Offerings that are sometimes referred to as "cult brands" also fit this category. Perhaps the best (and best-known) example is Harley Davidson, whose customers are regularly described by marketing scholars and business writers as fanatical. But having a niche product with great targeting is not enough to achieve the kind of loyalty Harley Davidson commands. Nor can it be achieved with friendly, courteous salespeople alone. Harley Davidson's focused front strategy includes numerous activities aimed at cementing the bond between the motorcycles and their riders. The company sponsors cross-country rides and has a thriving business selling branded apparel and a multitude of other goods. Through these additional customer-facing measures that are largely attractive only to its customer niche, Harley establishes what many commentators call a community of ownership.

PUTTING FRONT STRATEGY INTO PRACTICE

Once companies understand the dynamics of front-back strategy and have chosen a way of interacting with customers that fits with their long-term objectives, they need to think about implementation. One of the keys to successful implementation is understanding the proper deployment of people and technology to keep costs low, achieve crystal-clear focus, or obtain real differentiation in customer interactions.

Driving Radical Cost Leadership

Many companies will continue the trend of using technology to reduce the costs associated with customer interactions. They will increasingly engage in what is referred to euphemistically as "employing the customer." This is not a new trend: people have become used to getting their cash from automated teller machines and using push-button phones to get information from automated menus. But the pace of change is accelerating, as many people have become their own travel agents and in some retail outlets are scanning their own grocery purchases, bagging them, and paying for them with a credit or debit card.

Some management thinkers see such changes not as a shifting of burdens to customers but as more positive phenomena. They believe all business is moving to a place where the "co-creation of value" with customers will be the norm.[7] They see customer use of technologies such as the Internet fundamentally changing expectations and the nature of value creation in industries such as healthcare, where patients will bring vast amounts of their own research and other resources to their treatment. The fact remains, however, that certain costs will be transferred to customers, largely in the form of increased personal effort.

Some industries are finding they have no choice but to reduce face-to-face interactions by automating their customer-facing processes, especially in the face of increased demand and existing or expected labor shortages. Consider the pharmacy business, where demand for services is estimated to grow by 30 percent by 2007 but the number of pharmacists grows by only 6 percent.[8] Large chain pharmacies such as Rite-Aid (as noted by Jeffrey F. Rayport and Bernard J. Jaworski in *Best Face Forward: Why Companies Must Improve Their Service Interfaces with Customers*), and even smaller private chains such as Lewis Drug have recognized the danger that labor shortages pose to their business. They have already begun the shift to machine-led hybrids of customer service employees and technology, including using robots to fill prescriptions.[9] In what's known as a "central fill" facility, 4 pharmacists and 20 assistants can now fill 2,000 prescriptions a day, which are then distributed to retail outlets, versus the 100 prescriptions the average retail pharmacist is able to fill.[10]

Although companies may focus on developing low-cost front strategies, they are unlikely to secure an advantage for long. Imitation may be the sincerest form of flattery, but it is also the greatest threat that companies face in implementing front strategies effectively. Imitation by competitors is also why the correct front strategy must be aligned with a strong back strategy. Blockbuster is already threatening Netflix with its own online service offering, which it bolsters and differentiates by including a number of in-store rentals in the monthly subscription service fee. Retail giant Wal-Mart has likewise joined the fray. To stay in business, Netflix will have to constantly adapt to these significant threats.

As Michael Porter noted decades ago, when a company uses a technology that it did not develop (an "exogenous technology"), it rarely garners a significant first-mover advantage. Most of today's best customer-interface technologies are almost completely exogenous. Web interfaces, search capabilities, global positioning systems, and retail-store design software, to name just a few, are all technologies that companies now purchase or outsource to vendors to enable their customer interface solutions. Yet for the same reason of their easy accessibility to companies, they remain a competitive necessity. A low-cost front strategy will remain popular, but it will not on its own lead to high performance.

Achieving Laser-like Focus

When a company is attempting to implement a focused front strategy, the emphasis has to be on people over machines. The Ritz-Carlton hotel chain, for example, works to create a special connection with its customers through the intense special training its employees receive on how to interact with and treat guests. Employees learn, for example, that when guests ask directions to a location in the hotel, they should walk them there, not simply point them in the right direction.[11] Similarly, one-time affairs like Harley Davidson's "ride home" (in celebration of the company's 100th anniversary in 2003), which drew thousands of owners to events across the United States and abroad, also rely on people-to-people experiences to make them memorable.

But people are even more effective to companies that want to achieve focus when they are supported by technology. That's why many leading hotels capture data about customer preferences in computer files and distribute this information to their employees on a just-in-time basis. The systems allow the hotel chains to do much more than they could if they were relying on the memories and abilities of their employees, however well trained they may be. One hotel, for example, "remembered" a guest's love of gingerbread and was able to pleasantly surprise her by having the treat in her room when she returned for another stay, this time in a city 3,000 miles away.

Similarly, technology enables companies to undertake the complex calculations needed to determine who its Angel Customers are—insight that is ultimately acted on by people. Bankinter, one of Spain's top financial institutions, uses a continuous cycle of research, insight, and learning to increase its cross-selling ratios and the average value of its customers. The bank monitors transaction histories across its channels to know when to serve versus when to sell. Bankinter then uses this knowledge to deliver insights to customer-facing employees at the point of contact and to individualize automated customer interactions. Having a technology-enabled single view of the customer enables Bankinter to synchronize its customer relationship management strategy in all its channels, making employees in each channel more productive and effective.

Creating Real Differentiation

Achieving genuine differentiation in customer interactions is likely the hardest of the three front strategies to develop and implement. It requires companies to create distinctiveness by replicating an approach with many thousands of employees. It is difficult to hire or train in volume the kind of special employee who can provide distinctive customer experiences. Moreover, "scaling" an effective employee base often requires using technologies that are easily available or replicated, so it is not easy to maintain a competitive edge.

Many companies that get their successful start by developing distinctive human capital capabilities struggle as they grow. Home Depot built its initial success partly through its strategy of hiring savvy sales-floor employees, including former tradespeople and handy do-it-yourselfers.

As the company has expanded to employ more than 350,000 employees, including more than 160,000 new hires a year, however, finding such talent at high volume has become increasingly difficult.[12] Nordstrom's faces similar challenges in hiring large numbers of top-notch front-line employees.

Not surprisingly, some companies are turning to technology as a way of helping their people create real differentiation through their customer interactions. Front-line employees can treat more customers in a special way when technology gives them knowledge and lets them apply it immediately. Technologies are being developed that allow shop-floor salespeople to see where customers are located and how long they have studied certain items. These new technologies also give salespeople instant information about those items (their competitive and available features) to help them more quickly and accurately assist customers. Major retailers are now using similar technologies to create differentiated sales and service performance "at scale."

MAKING AN ACTIVE CHOICE

With so much change in technology today, the need to understand customer interactions from the perspective of strategy is greater than ever. Executives should resist the temptation to spend money on customers that can't be justified by the returns on investment. Rather, they should make a conscious choice to seek cost leadership, differentiation, or focus in their customer interaction strategy. When paired with an overall strategy based on a sound assessment of the business's industry position and distinctive capabilities, a carefully developed front strategy should help the company find a viable competitive advantage.

And when front-line employees are part of a well-honed customer-interaction strategy, it's much easier for them to make quick decisions that align with company strategy. In other words, they'll have a much better idea of how to calibrate the relationship between efficiency and personal service. They may not be able to make all customers happy in every circumstance, but they will have a solid understanding of why, sometimes, that's okay.

NOTES

The authors thank David A. Light, the Accenture Institute for High Performance Business's editor, for his assistance with this chapter.

1. Leonard L. Berry, Lewis P. Carbone, and Stephan H. Haeckel, "Managing the Total Customer Experience," *MIT Sloan Management Review*," Spring (2002): 85–89.

2. Mylene Mangalindan, "Amazon Net Falls as Rivals Take Toll," *Wall Street Journal* (April 27, 2005): A3.

3. "Upscale Car Dealerships Rolling out All the Perks," *Atlanta Business Journal* (June 4, 2004): A2.

4. Gary Loveman, " Diamonds in the Data Mine," *Harvard Business Review* (May 2003): 109–113.

5. Gary McWilliams and Steven Gray, "Slimming Down Stores," *Wall Street Journal* (April 29, 2005): B1; Erin McCarthy, "The Chance to Escape," *ddimagazine.com*, March 1, 2005.

6. Douglas B. Holt, *How Brands Become Icons: The Principles of Cultural Branding* (Harvard Business School Press, 2004).

7. C.K. Prahalad and Venkat Ramaswamy, *The Future of Competition: Co-creating Unique Value with Customers* (Cambridge. Harvard Business School Press, 2004).

8. Jeffrey F. Rayport and Bernard J. Jaworski, *Best Face Forward: Why Companies Must Improve Their Service Interfaces with Customers* (Cambridge: Harvard Business School Press, 2005).

9. Jay Kirschenmann, "High-tech Drug-Order Filling, Private Ownership Lend Edge," *Argus Leader* (Sioux Falls, S. Dak.) May 18, 2003; see also, Rayport and Jaworski, op. cit.

10. Mya Frazier, "RX for Drugstores: Chains Turning to Automation, Technicians To Reduce Costs and Answer Shortage of Pharmacists," *Cleveland Plain Dealer*, September 11, 2001.

11. See Jeffrey F. Rayport and Bernard J. Jaworski, *Best Face Forward: Why Companies Must Improve Their Service Interfaces with Customers*, op. cit., for additional discussion.

12. Milt Freudenheim, "More Help Wanted: Older Workers Please Apply," *New York Times*, March 23, 2005.

CHAPTER 3

What Charles Taught Me about Trust at the Front Line

Robert M. Galford and Woodruff W. Driggs

Much of my work focuses on the topic of building trusted relationships—sometimes between professionals and their clients, and sometimes between corporate leaders and their employees. Much of it takes place with highly paid executives and professionals in financial services and similar disciplines.

I often ask these leaders and managers to describe what their relationships with others in the organization might look like if trust was a "given." Sometimes, they're hard-pressed to do so, and they throw the question back at me, looking for a "for example" to help them jog their thinking.

When they do, I talk about Charles.

I was in New Orleans, technically "off-duty" at the time, in that my trip was not business related. My travel companion was our then 17-year-old daughter Katy, and the business at hand was looking at colleges for the next year. She was treating this with great seriousness, and with only one night to spend in the area, she was determined not to waste an opportunity with anything ordinary, in either accommodations or dining. I was only too happy to indulge her, and while our luxury hotel in the French Quarter offered us a pleasant but unspectacular experience, our dinner with Charles Carter was nothing short of remarkable.

I had called an old friend who was a New Orleans regular for restaurant advice. A graduate of the local university and law school, her connection to New Orleans remains strong a quarter-century later, even though she is now a partner in a major New York law firm. "With only one night in town, you've got to go to Antoine's, and you really ought to book reservations through your waiter. Call my family's waiter, D——, and use my name." Which I did. Quickly. D—— wasn't in when I called, but I was told that my message would be put in his file for our upcoming visit.

Fast forward several weeks later. A rainy, somewhat unpleasant weeknight in New Orleans. Antoine's front room was quiet, almost empty. I felt silly having called for reservations. To make matters worse, when we arrived, we were told that D—— wasn't working that night, but that "Charles will be taking care of you." I have to confess to feeling a small pang of disappointment at the news, having prepared both Katy and myself for the likelihood of royal treatment under the care of D—— as a result of having invoked my friend's name upon the reservation. My initial disappointment was compounded when we were introduced to Charles. He looked to be just about Katy's age. Strike one for being tended to by one of the vaunted long-established waiters. We were escorted out of the front room and into the back. Strike two, I thought.

Here's how wrong I was. Charles Carter took better care of us than any waiter I can remember in some four decades as a food-obsessed adult. He turned a good meal at Antoine's into a truly memorable experience, not just for me, but for Katy, who even at the tender age of 18 has had her share of some pretty good dining. Twenty-two years old, Charles was the son of an Antoine's waiter with a 30+ year tenure and the great-nephew of a waiter who began his career at Antoine's in 1928.

Charles showed us photographs and news clippings dating back 40 years and more, featuring his great-uncle who was "privileged" (his word) to be one of the waiters to have served the presidents, popes, and royalty who had dined at Antoine's in the past. He was attentive, graceful, never obsequious, and fully charming. With seven years of Antoine's experience under his belt, Charles pointed out the other waiters in the dining room full of regulars under whom he had trained, and described how he had moved up the hierarchy from busboy to assistant waiter, and now to a full-status waiter. He pointed with pride to the fellow (clearly older than himself) he himself had trained, who was now working in the dining room (and in Charles' own words, was "doing very well").

Yet somehow, in all of this, the experience was never about Charles. He made it about us. He politely asked what brought us to New Orleans and turned the mention of Tulane University into a wonderful tableau, describing how the Tulane seniors would come to dinner at Antoine's as part of the graduation ritual, and how they would fill the room. Katy asked me whether I would come visit every month if she ended up at Tulane so that Charles could be our regular waiter.

But it didn't end there. It was the same process step-by-step through the meal. Never obtrusive, but always present. Comments on the menu, suggestions on what to try, little samples brought on the side. Never pushy, but apparently sincere in such suggestions as not to miss a special dessert or a special coffee.

Charles was less of a waiter and more of a gracious host. He took us on a behind the scenes tour, showing us the restaurant's memorabilia and explaining the various aspects of New Orleans society and establishment families. We stopped in briefly at the kitchen, where, along with another round of introductions, we shook hands with the woman "who made your dessert." We have no idea whether Charles gave the same treatment to all he served, whether he let us in on any secrets that were really not otherwise public, or whether he was showing and telling us things that his management would have rather kept private. In truth, it really doesn't matter. We felt included, cared about, special.

What does matter, however, is what can be learned from our visit to Antoine's, and whether those lessons can take hold in environments that are not as steeped in generations of service, or are structured for extensive behind the scenes tours for all comers. Here are a few hypotheses about what can be learned, and about translating the lessons across a broader landscape:

Pride of place and pride in one's work can be developed among employees, even if you're not Antoine's. I saw this recently at our local Whole Foods Market, where I have now run into not one, but two cashiers whom I knew from previous stints at other local food stores. One of them had been a long-time presence at the local gourmet store, the other at a local farm market. When I spoke with each of them, they were effusive in their praise of their new employer—as an employer, as a food provider, and so on. Previously, I would not have described either one of them as go-go, rah-rah types as workers. Now, a complete transformation, with two employees who wax eloquent about their "team" and the products they sell.

The challenge for all employers, whether their workforce is composed of skilled professionals or seasonal workers, is to take what makes them proud of where they work and instill a similar pride in the people at the front line. The challenge for top managers is to ensure that front-line managers (who hire the front-line employees) feel like "employers" in this sense.

Aside from the prospects receiving a nice, regular paycheck, there's a reason why you joined your company. You liked what they did, or how they did it, or who ran it, or who worked there. Assuming your judgment was pretty good (if it wasn't, presumably, you'd either be looking to leave or long gone), you can and should convey those sentiments to those working for you.

Trust has to be built and conveyed on three levels: strategic, organizational, and individual. Do front-line employees believe in the organization's mission, strategies, products, and the like? If they do, they have strategic trust. But strategic trust is often hard to develop among front-line employees, especially those who perform tasks that seem isolated from the intangibles of strategy (cashiers positions, for example). Waiting tables is often similarly isolated (although an employee can have faith in the product at hand); however, Charles is living proof that the connection can be made. I didn't ask Charles about strategy or mission per se, but his knowledge of both was apparent in his grasp of the restaurant's place among competitors, in New Orleans, and in history.

Charles was also an exemplar of organizational trust, or trust in the systems and processes under which the company functions. These may include operating systems, manufacturing processes, and the like, but it's really more than that. It's *how things get done.* Are employees treated fairly? Do promotions or evaluations take place when scheduled? Are raises given as promised? Are rewards fairly allocated? The answers to all of those questions (and more) are the indicia—and the foundations—of organizational trust.

Finally, Charles clearly possessed individual trust—that is, trust in the people he works for and with. Charles didn't hesitate to take us "backstage" at Antoine's; he didn't hesitate to provide food samples; he had complete confidence that what he was doing was acceptable and integral to the establishment. He expected that the people with whom he worked would share that confidence as well, and they did. Witness the ease of manner of the woman who made our desserts; she wasn't surprised, or disturbed, to see him with diners in tow. She trusted what he was doing; he had faith in her response.

Ask yourself: Do the people working for you trust you? Do you trust them? What about your managers at the local level? Do they trust their employees and vice versa? What would it be like if there were high levels of trust between managers and employees throughout your company, and what would it take to get there?

Building any sort of trust with employees requires the leaders (and managers, in turn) to perform against five very specific criteria: clear aspirations, resources and capabilities, follow-through, alignment, and articulation.

You can quickly design and administer a "Would Charles Believe This about Our Workplace?" test. Here's how. Pick someone in your organization who is operating at the front line, like a Charles, and ask yourself (or even better, ask that person) whether he or she would be able to vouch for your management group's performance on these dimensions:

1. *Clear aspirations.* What is the company striving to achieve for its customers, its shareholders, and its employees?
2. *Resources and capabilities.* Does the entity actually have a chance of achieving those aspirations? Doing so requires a set of abilities and resources—skill-sets, tools, and technologies among them. It's tough to have employees cut sandwiches if

there aren't enough knives, or they aren't sharpened, or folks don't know how to handle them. It's tough to have Charles be a cheerleader for Antoine's if he doesn't learn how to tell the stories that charm customers. A colleague of mine recently reported that as she was selecting ground beef at the supermarket, an employee came out from the back room and asked, "Are you finding what you need?" She said, "I think so," but then followed up with a question: "Can you tell me the difference between the meat that simply says "angus" on the label, and the meat that says "Coleman?" He shook his head, and said, "No, I really don't know." She moved on, shaking her head. "If he doesn't know, why ask if he can help?"

3. *Following through with actions.* From the point of view of your front-line employees, does your organization just talk about being number one, or does it actually do anything? Does it ever try new things? Consider how, in its constant need for more staff, Home Depot formed an alliance with the American Association of Retired Persons to create (and recruit for) a "snowbirds" program that permits people to work in the northern part of the United States in the temperate months, and to work in Florida in the winters.

4. Making sure that the requirements placed on workers by one part of the organization are aligned with those introduced by other parts of the organization. If Charles had felt pressure to "turn the tables" a certain number of times an evening, he might not have felt free to deliver the level of service he did. If Charles had been serving a greater number of tables, he might have had to curtail his efforts on our behalf. While it's important to teach employees in general how to deal with ambiguity or competing demands, foisting such conflict on them can push them quickly to a point of diminishing returns. Consider the employee who is told that he or she is empowered to "go the extra mile" for customers, but who is chastised if he or she does so. Balancing ambiguity can place too much of a burden on people in the workforce who are not equipped, trained, or rewarded to cope with those kinds of conflicts. Dealing with ambiguity is a management-level task, and the greater the ambiguity, the better off we are in holding managers and executives accountable.

5. Making sure that the desired aspirations, abilities, actions are not just well aligned, but *well articulated* across the organization. One of the challenges of getting employees to do what managers say is making sure that the message is clear, consistent, and continuous. I'm constantly surprised by how surprised managers are that their message hasn't gotten through. "But I've told them that!" they say. And it's true. They have. Once. Maybe even more. Maybe in a speech. Maybe at a town meeting. Maybe in an e-mail. Maybe in a newsletter. It doesn't matter. We all know that the great brands and the great messages get advertised to us again and again, over and over, in multiple forms. And the expenditures for message reinforcement or "getting the point across" rarely go down. Nor should they. It's pretty clear that Charles has an advantage in this area by being a third-generation employee; no doubt he has had a share of input and/or interpretation regarding the company from family members. But Antoine's managers must be doing a good job of articulation as well, to keep the message clear and up –to date over the years.

Nothing matters in these situations more than individual trust, and specifically the level of trust in the relationship between the employee and his or her direct supervisor. This is true no matter how far up (or down) the ladder you go, whether we're talking about the CEO and his or her Executive Vice Presidents, or the crew chief and the front line at the fast-food franchise.

I recently had the occasion to conduct a series of intensive one-on-one interviews with the General Managers in charge of the various regions of one of America's more prominent companies. The firm is a 100-year old company with the largest market share in one of the country's largest industries. The particular issue at hand was the general manager/business leader role itself, how it was scoped, its challenges and rewards, and even the nature of the relationship between the region and the corporate headquarters functions.

After having spent roughly two hours each with 10 of these individuals, it was clear to me that the level of job satisfaction (and arguably the potential for success) in that role was more a function of the quality of the relationship between each general manager (GM) and his direct superior (a corporate EVP) than any other variable that one might identify. In those situations where there was deep trust in the EVP expressed by the GM, the inevitable frustrations of the job were considered manageable. Where there was less trust or less familiarity with their EVP, GMs were far more critical about the burdens of the role. There is a lifeline relationship between worker and supervisor, regardless of how high up the hierarchy you go. Those who feel nurtured and supported feel that they can work through the problems. Even if they are talented, those who lack that nurturance and support (or have a negative impression of their superiors) are either unlikely to make it, or are unlikely to try and stick it out.

I guess that's the final message of our visit with Charles Carter. While Charles deserves all the credit he gets for his skill and his style, we should leave a little bit of credit for his bosses at Antoine's as well, for they are the ones who turned him into a star at the tender age of 22.

And, oh, by the way, in the end, Katy chose not to go to Tulane. I think her biggest regret in doing so was the fact we wouldn't dine regularly with Charles Carter.

NOTE

Antoine's re-opened for business, post-Hurricane Katrina, in December 2005.

CHAPTER 4

A Mission for the Front Line

Edward E. Lawler III

Almost every company I know has a mission statement. Some are ignored and of no more value than the paper they are written on. The best are valuable in a directional sense. They can serve to focus or center the company on an overarching goal.

Even the best, however, often don't affect front-line employee behavior. Generated at the highest levels of the company and broadly strategic in nature, they do not mean much in a practical sense to the people who are paid the least yet have the most contact with customers.

And that's too bad, because the benefits of front-line employees having a meaningful mission can be enormous. When employees have a mission they can articulate and accept, they have a raison d'être at work. The job becomes more than the sum of the tasks to be done, however mundane those tasks might be.

That's why individual store locations would do well to generate their own missions. Every small branch of every nationwide chain—in fact, every department in every department store, every franchise location, every big box, small box, premium or discount arena in which front-line employees interact with customers at the point-of-purchase—should have its own mission.

The local mission should *complement* the mission of the organization at large. Obviously, it can't be at odds with the direction of the company as a whole. But beyond that, there's room for a lot of creativity. The only critical requirement is that it be meaningful for the people it is intended to motivate.

That means it can't be too vague or "pie in the sky." It's great when a mission can focus on a "better humanity" type of goal; no one disputes the motivation that many employees in nonprofits get out of working for a worthy cause. But an effective mission has to link, in a clear way, to the work at hand. To that end, it can be as simple as "Our grocery store is going to be cleaner and easier to navigate than XYZ grocery store down the street," or, "We're going to offer the best service in Boston."

Unromantic? Mundane? To you, maybe. But consider the tasks of the front-line employees in your company. What do they do all day, every day? Can you establish a clear connection between their jobs and the overall mission of your company? A local mission might be the missing link.

SELECTING THE RIGHT MISSION

Research that I did together with J. Richard Hackman[1] revealed three critical job characteristics that lead to more motivated employees:

1. The experience of work being *meaningful*
2. The experience of *responsibility* for results
3. *Feedback* or knowledge of results.

Missions are an important building block for all three of these characteristics. A mission by nature provides meaning. A mission gives people a reason to take on responsibility and to be invested in the outcomes of their work. A mission also can provide a good way to benchmark results in a local and immediate manner (so as to have more meaning for front-line employees) than corporate results might have.

What is the right mission for your front-line employees and the team with whom they work? Should you aim to "one-up" a local competitor? Should you compete with other units of your own organization? Should your mission focus on customer satisfaction? Should it focus on bringing in new customers?

If your overall goal in identifying a mission for your own locale is to create an environment in which front-line employees are motivated to work harder, or better, or interact more productively with customers, then your mission-to-select-a-mission should start with the criteria that make for meaningful work.

A more detailed look at the first two conditions that motivate employees can also provide an excellent way for managers to identify possible missions and select the best one for his or her team.[2]

Consider:

Meaningfulness. Does the job involve doing a "whole" or "complete" task? That is, can the employee say "I did that," or "We did that" and point to an in-store initiative or customer interaction he or she can take complete responsibility for? In manufacturing jobs, where employees often contribute one piece of a whole product, this is often difficult, if not impossible, to achieve. But in sales and service positions, a little redesign can sometimes allow employees to engage in something "start to finish," whether it is a product display, a customer interaction that goes from question to sale, or a special project that they designed with managerial approval or input.

Does the work involve doing a "significant" task? In other words, does the task contribute to the store's ability to fulfill its goals in a tangible and visible way? Is it something that other workers can appreciate? Is it something customers might comment on?

Does the work call for the employee to use valued skills, valued meaning skills the employee can identify and be proud of, and skills that they alone may excel at? These skills do not have to be related to level of formal education. When an employee has a knack for doing something, and a manager can showcase that talent, an opportunity exists for increased motivation on the job.

The characteristics of a meaningful job are subjective. What is meaningful to one employee may not resonate in the same way with another. There is also a fine line, particularly in lower-paying jobs, between "showcasing" an employee's particular strengths and asking that employee to do work that is eventually perceived as being "extra" or "burdensome." But the upside potential is great enough that the risk is worth taking, if the manager is willing to provide the kind of support for the other two conditions (responsibility and feedback) that helps sustain enriched jobs in front-line settings. It is important to ask employees what their reactions are to their task and work. Their answers can provide useful guidance when it comes to identifying tasks they find to be meaningful, and they are also the best sources of information about what skills they value.

Responsibility. Do employees have freedom regarding how their work gets done? Can they determine the order of tasks? Can they operate without close supervision, in at least part of their job? When someone is being monitored and directed all the time, it can be easy to lose interest in trying to excel on a personal basis. The employee's view can quickly change from "I'm going to try to get this right because I want to do well," to "I'm going to try to get this right because I'm being watched" to "It's not my fault if I get something wrong. What's the point of trying to get it right when I'm going to be corrected at every turn anyway?" Further, when closely directed, employees don't "own the results" because they didn't have control; their supervisor did.

It's often difficult to allow front-line employees any significant amount of freedom. Particularly in organizations where the product is formulaic and the process must be strictly followed to produce the product (fast-food franchises, or customer service call centers, for example). But even in these situations, there is some room for the kind of creativity that can create autonomy. Frito Lay, for example, carefully measures sales results and customer satisfaction (its local mission is integral to the organization's mission, in that sense), but it also gives salespeople a great deal of freedom when it comes to dealing with the individual managers of stores that carry their chips, regarding where and how the project is displayed.

Take a relatively simple "local" mission: "Our grocery store is going to be cleaner and easier to navigate than XYZ grocery store down the street." How does that play out in practice? How does a store manager know if his or her mission is taking root and taking off?

Measurements come into play here, not only to track the success of the idea, but also (and most important) to give employees something tangible that reflects their progress. The parent company no doubt imposes financial performance standards that must be met; that's not what I'm talking about here.

I am talking about "mission measures" that are positive ways to track mission success. The manager might start by brainstorming with employees about how the mission might be fulfilled. What kinds of changes would have to be made? If one "forgot" the existing processes and policies, what might "success" look like? How would we know we were succeeding? What could we measure?

It is hoped that a few ideas would emerge that the manager could then "test market" for a few weeks. Then he or she could return to the employees and ask. Is this working? How well? How might it be made better? What might we add to this initiative? In this way, local approaches to local missions can be created and refined.

Which brings me to *feedback*—the third condition required for an enriched job. Most organizations have established and formal routes for performance feedback. In the best scenarios, employees receive feedback, which is a carefully designed mix of input from peers, bosses, and customers. Measuring the progress of a local mission can dovetail nicely with those formal performance management processes; it can also enhance them.

Bear in mind: mission feedback, as with any kind of feedback, can often come in the form of silence (particularly from peers and customers). A local mission—say the mission of an ice-cream shop in a tourist area—might be "We're going to be the cleanest ice-cream parlor in the town." Reduced complaints about the state of the restrooms at that ice-cream parlor can either mean that customers have given up complaining (unlikely), or that the restroom is up to par to the extent that it no longer registers on customers' radars. It is a "given" part of the expected standard of service.

Wait time for customer service is another such example. When customers don't have long to wait, employees (and managers) generally don't hear about it. But when the wait time is long, or perceived as being unfair, they do.

Consider one Mother's Day rush at a popular Italian restaurant chain. When one family of four arrived and put their name on the wait list, they were sixth in line for a four-top or a booth. The hostess had said the wait would be about 15 minutes, but it soon dragged into 30, then 40 minutes. After inquiring about the wait, the family was told that the wait wouldn't be too much longer, and that there were a number of parties just finishing up their meals. Fair enough. Then the family became aware that the restaurant, which does not take reservations, was in fact allowing customers to call in, put their name on the list, and then drive to the establishment, so as to minimize their wait. Again, fair enough. But then one of the phone-in families showed up, and complained loudly when they found that their table was not yet ready. They, too, had been told 15 minutes. Fielding the complaint, the hostess bumped them to the head of the line and sat them almost immediately. The first family then complained, calling the process unfair, and they too were seated immediately. Predictably, this set off a storm among the other families still waiting for tables.

The front-line employees experienced a rare problem that Mother's Day, mishandled it in the clutch, and heard about it publicly from customers and from their manager, who had to step in to soothe the customers still in line. Yet the restaurant is generally known for its prompt service. Do these employees ever receive positive feedback on nights when everything goes smoothly?

One final example of an opportunity for mission feedback: Being on time for work should be a baseline requirement of employment, and peers may not comment if an employee is on time consistently. But if an employee's on-time record may represent a significant improvement over previous performance levels, that's an improvement worth noting. It is up to the managers to seek out these "positives in disguise" and recognize them explicitly.

MINING THE FRONT LINES FOR INFORMATION

Some of the best ideas for achieving local missions and for encouraging the development of a virtuous spiral at work come from the front-line employees themselves. But getting at those ideas can be difficult.

Asking for written suggestions doesn't often work well. Front-line employees sometimes feel they don't have the time to write down their thoughts; they may also be fearful of doing anything as formal as putting something in writing.

One alternative is to form a problem-solving group led by a manager, with several employees on board. Another is to hold a meeting at which employees can brainstorm ideas. (The first meeting might not generate much, but the second might, and the manager might also find that employees contribute ideas on a one-to-one basis, in the days that follow.)

Managers can also study the local competition and urge their employees to do the same. They can ask for reports back: What did you see? What do they do? Could we do something like that? Could we do better?

Finally, gathering data from customers can be a natural role for frontline employees. In the course of their interactions with customers, they can ask: What do you like about the store? What would you like to see more of? Less of? A quick conversation can yield insights that contribute directly to the formation and fulfillment of a local mission.

NOTES

1. J.R. Hackman and E.E. Lawler III, "Employee Reactions to Job Characteristics," *Journal of Applied Psychology* 55 (1971): 259–286.

2. Edward E. Lawler III, *Treat People Right* (San Francisco: Jossey-Bass, 2003): 142.

CHAPTER 5

The Case for the Chief Experience Officer

Jeffrey F. Rayport

Everyone has had the experience: You see an item in a department store catalog and decide to buy it from the store because it's on your way home from work. But the retail clerk in the store cannot locate the item in the store and, after looking in the store's product database, the clerk tells you it does not exist. At home you turn to your PC, find the online site, locate the product, and order it, but now you must wait to have it delivered. You get the result you sought, but not in the way you wanted it.

Similarly, you search for a car online, you compare features and performance across the models you like, and you zero in on the specific vehicle that meets your needs. With the auto maker's online site, you configure the exact car you want, you even price it, and you send the information to a local dealer. At first, you get no response. You were expecting an e-mail confirming a time to visit the dealer and test drive the car; instead, a dealership sales person calls and leaves a message with only a name and phone number. You schedule a test drive by phone, which takes several more calls, only to go to the dealership and find that the car you specified isn't there. In fact, no one has any information about the car you requested in your e-mail. Although the search process was efficient, you must start again at square one.

Similarly, you dial your credit card issuer, and the automated voice-response system requests that you enter your 17-digit account number, which you do. After a wait, along with repeated recordings warmly telling you how much your card company values your business and how deeply the company respects you and the value of your time, a live customer service representative comes on the line and asks for your account number. You said you already entered it; she tells you that the system did not forward the information. And you start again.

In each case, the problem is the same. The combination of people and technology deployed across multiple service channels has failed to provide the *basic* service experience you sought or required, let alone the world-class service experience you expected. Yet service pathologies of this kind hardly represent isolated instances. There's not a reader of this book, I suspect, who would fail to identify with one or more of the preceding scenarios. Recent research findings explain why. As companies have gone to heroic lengths to field multiple service channels to meet customers' needs most effectively—ranging from brick-and-mortar stores to catalogs, Web sites, call centers, interactive voice-response units (IVRs), and kiosks, to name a few—customers have become more frustrated than ever because of a lack of coordination and consistency of experience across those touch points. Indeed, judging from the American Customer Satisfaction Index (ACSI), customer satisfaction has remained flat or has declined even as costs of service have risen. In a study of 176 corporations with annual revenues over $500 million in North America by Forrester Research, only 27 percent of the sample fulfilled 80 percent of the basic criteria for providing an integrated cross-channel experience.[1] When executives at these corporations were asked to name their greatest obstacles to improving customer experience, 73 percent selected "getting alignment across [internal] organizations" as their greatest barrier.[2] Perhaps it should come as no surprise to learn that less than one-fourth of the companies in the survey placed authority over all customer touch points in the hands of a single executive.[3]

CUSTOMER EXPERIENCE MEETS COMPLEX SYSTEMS

So what's going on? Think of a corporation as a complex human and technological system. From a customer's point of view, most companies lack a compelling and comprehensive version of what technologists call a "presentation layer." This is the interface that makes an operating system visually compelling and user-friendly (think Windows versus DOS) or the interface that makes the Internet so easy to navigate that nontechnologists can use it (think World Wide Web or AOL versus BITNET and USENET). Firms, when large-scale and complex, require presentation layers. Indeed, without integration of interfaces or touch points into an appropriately configured presentation layer, a company's offerings (its products and services) and its operations (its people, organization, and processes) appear to act in ways that make no sense to customers and present a corporate "face" that's difficult for customers to understand.

Consult the Web site of just about any major corporation—from American Express to AT&T, from Microsoft to IBM—and try to find an answer to a relevant question or address a relevant need. You will be greeted by a seemingly blinding array of product choices and options, with no clear way to use the site to access the specific services or information you need. Even when a corporation directs you with a promotion to a specific location within a site, you may have similar problems. When Motorola introduced its new camera phone in 2004, the V710, it bought glossy inserts in upscale magazines such as *Vanity Fair* and *The New Yorker* to invite readers to go online to access a special offer for its sleek, innovative handset. It also sent out a targeted e-mail campaign to attract a similarly upscale audience to its new device. But when recipients of these advertising messages went online, they found only an area of Motorola's site with general information on mobile phones and no sign of the new model. In addition, a search on the site for the V710 yielded no results. It turned out that Motorola's marketers had rolled out their campaign in the absence of a product ready for market!

In orchestrating customer experience, companies cannot expect customers to learn the arcane navigation of a corporation's systems and subsystems, any more than a software package could prove successful if customers had to use "machine language" to access its functionality. Nor can a company expect customers to perform the work of integrating the elements of its offerings. The combination of poor presentation layer and poor internal integration of functions in technology systems creates inferior experiences for users. When similar ills afflict companies and the users are customers, bad things happen. In the beginning, customers become dissatisfied. Ultimately, they go away.

In an era characterized by less intense competition, the question of how well companies present themselves to customers and markets might not qualify as strategic. But these days, with too many firms and too many offerings competing for too few customers, it's easy to conclude that companies are having an ever more difficult time establishing offering-based sources of advantage. What was once true only for the computer and consumer electronics industries—compressed product lifecycles, an accelerating Moore's law, rapid-cycle commoditization—is now a dynamic that afflicts practically every industry that depends on (and is driven by) information technology, including retail, transportation, hospitability, media and entertainment, and automotive, to name just a few. The tyranny of what Stan Shih, the founder of Acer Computer, called a decade ago the "three-six-one" product lifecycle (three months to develop a differentiated offering, six months to sell it profitably at an elevated price point, and one month to liquidate excess inventory after it becomes a commodity) has become the rule, not the exception, across a wide range of industries.

That means that corporate innovation focused only on core product or service offerings is necessary but not sufficient to ensure competitive advantage in the long term. Innovation must also focus on how companies go to market (what we have elsewhere described as "demand-side innovation")—a focus on how they structure relationships with customers, how they manage the interfaces that enable those relationships, and how they evolve operating and economic models to meet changing customer needs. In this sense, sustainable advantage is built increasingly on a new frontier that's defined by how well firms manage interactions and relationships with customers and markets. When those interactions and relationships are sufficiently satisfying and loyalty-inducing, companies can keep customers despite compressed product lifecycles, downward pricing pressures, and disruptions to underlying technologies. When interactions generate dissatisfied customers, companies forfeit their future. This is what makes the difference between great brands, which transcend the fate of individual product or service offerings (think Nike or Intel), and those that live and die based on the often short-term viability of what they have to sell (think Ford and General Motors). This is the new frontier at which a move in service quality up or down will make or break great corporations.

WHY SYSTEMS THINKING MATTERS

We can state the problem succinctly: Companies have come to resemble complex systems, which require astutely designed presentation layers to make them intelligible to customers. Yet, those presentation layers are composed of touch points characterized by insufficient optimization (for example, a confusing corporate Web site) and insufficient coordination, consistency, and integration (for example, lack of alignment across service channels), resulting in an overall degradation of customer experience. To make matters worse, a proliferation of touch points has made management of corporate interfaces increasingly costly and complex, and it has put pressure on nearly every function within large corporations to conceive of its operations differently. For example, marketers must now align their media "mixes" with heretofore unrelated corporate activities such as product design, operations, and customer service. Managers may question whether all of these elements constitute part of a firm's "face" to the external world, but customers make no such distinctions. Every touch point manages in important, often strategic, ways the attitudes and behaviors of customers and markets. That's why we call the sum total of the interfaces that link a company to its customers and markets an "interface system."

Someone must manage the interface system to achieve outstanding customer service and customer experience. Otherwise, no one is driving optimization of or coordination across interfaces, and no one is raising the obvious questions. For example, successful brands, especially in services, translate their core promises and values into actions at each and every touch point. Recent history among the ailing air carriers illustrates the risks of failing to make such translation into reality. When United Airlines urged customers in its advertising "To fly the friendly skies," or Delta Airlines similarly claimed, "We love to fly, and it shows," each slogan had implications for the attitudes and behaviors of ticketing agents, gate personnel, and cabin staff. Each also implied differences in brochures and collateral such as ticket jackets, in frequent flyer programs, in airline club lounges, and in service environments more generally. Of course, both United and Delta failed to achieve such alignment across marketing and service interfaces. Consequently, the campaigns managed to raise customer expectations (as "United Rising" continues to do today), only to underwhelm them with substandard performance.

With today's complexity of service delivery systems, translating brand promises into specific managerial actions involving front-line service workers and automated service interfaces becomes ever more important. When brand promises suggest specific attitudes and behaviors, the translation may occur more readily. For example, Niketown stores reflect Nike's "Just do it" ethos in the recruiting and selection of athletically oriented sales personnel, the use of inspiring sound and visual imagery in the retail environment, and the performance focus of the merchandise in each of its sport-specific product lines. But when brand promises are more abstract and atmospheric, the difficulty of making the translation into action increases. For example, how such financial services institutions as UBS ("You and Us") or Royal Bank of Scotland ("Make it happen") will translate their brand messages into specific actions across an array of human and machine interfaces will be an interesting story to watch.

THE CASE FOR THE CHIEF EXPERIENCE OFFICER

All of this begs the question: In corporations today, who takes responsibility for interfaces and interface systems? Who is accountable for the optimization of each interface on a stand-alone basis and for orchestration and integration of the system as a whole? Who ultimately ensures that the interface system creates satisfying loyalty-inducing customer experiences? In most companies, it's either the CEO, or it's no one at all. Because the CEO already has a day job, neither is a very good answer.

To ensure desired customer experiences, smart companies will appoint Chief Experience Officers. Call this individual the "other" CEO—or, what we prefer, the CXO.

The strategic agenda of the CXO starts with a line of inquiry focused on how the enterprise is configured to manage its interfaces and combine them into a coherent interface system. In just about every company that competes on service or relationships, such questioning can highlight enormously daunting "internal" issues related to a company's organizational structure and governance, management incentives, and enterprise economics. To begin, the CXO must ask:

- Have we deployed the right interfaces in the right places at the right times in the right ways—and have we too many interfaces or too few?
- Have we optimized each of our interfaces according to targeted customers' preferences and needs, by segment and usage occasion?
- Have we understood the "pathways" our customers define as they flow through our interfaces in purchase or repurchase processes?
- Have we aligned and integrated those interfaces (along with the people, processes, and activities that support them) into consistent and coordinated systems to enable coherent customer experiences?

Of course, you could argue that this as an old story. After all, many companies, industrial or otherwise, have long relied on multiple service channels to compete. But something else is happening that is upping the ante for getting this right. That's the emerging opportunity for what we call "front-office reengineering." As leading firms find ways to substitute capital for labor in the front office where services are delivered, they are engaged in a reengineering effort that is analogous to the automation and process redesign revolutions that transformed agriculture in the nineteenth century, manufacturing in the twentieth century, and corporate information processing only a few decades ago.

THE MARRIAGE OF PEOPLE AND MACHINES

In recent years, new types of machine interfaces have emerged to play unprecedented roles in automating interactions with customers. In the 1970s, the ATM provided an alternative to bank tellers; as attractive as ATMs became to retail banking customers, few people considered ATMs true customer relationship managers. ATMs were all about efficiency. Contrast that to how we feel today about automated interfaces at Web sites such as Amazon and Google, to electronic devices such as iPod and TiVo, to virtual agents such as Amtrak's Julie, Canada Bell's Emily, or AT&T's TellMe. Each of these is an automated service interface that's sufficiently intelligent, interactive, engaging, and networked so that it transcends a functional role and appeals to users in meaningful and, at times, emotionally compelling ways.

Emotional responses to automated interfaces signal new possibilities for the roles machines can play in the front-line workforce. Affective technologies can enable more effective interchange between companies and customers, while reducing the costs of each transaction or interaction. Whereas past reengineering efforts focused on efficiency, front-office reengineering focuses on efficiency *and* effectiveness. Front-office reengineering comprises three fundamental impacts on the design of work: *substitution* (machines for labor), *complementarity* (machines in combination with labor), and *displacement* (outsourcing or off-shoring of machines or labor). It is out of these choices that optimized interfaces and "interface systems" emerge and open up new frontiers of efficiency and effectiveness for large-scale corporations in interacting with customers.

Such implications buttress the argument for the creation of a new C-suite role: Ultimately, firms that aspire to get their interface systems right will change their enterprise economics by (often radically) reengineering the way services are delivered, jobs are defined, and incentives are structured. In the process, they will render obsolete many of the ways corporations are organized today, by driving integration not around functions or business units but around customers—with a focus on who their customers are (their personas), the experiences they desire (their chosen pathways through the purchase process), and their expectations of corporate brands (the brand promise).

Consider a case in point—the quick-serve restaurant industry. In recent years, McDonald's has sought a variety of ways to improve its diminished standing in service rankings among fast-food brands. In the past, much of the chain's innovation focused on menu innovations, some tailored to local tastes (the Mandise in France, sushi in Japan), most designed at headquarters and rolled out across the system (Egg McGriddle). With more than 30,000 stores around the world, it was only a matter of time before McDonald's would look to service innovation to improve the chain's brand standing. Today, McDonald's has experimented with order-entry kiosks (substituting touch-screen terminals for cash register operators) and a host of other automated ordering systems. The most intriguing is a plan to move drive-thru order-entry, which accounts for roughly half of store sales, from the kitchens into call centers serving clusters of restaurant units. This move, facilitated by low costs of network connectivity, has made order processing for drive-thru more accurate and more pleasant for customers, while creating more agreeable jobs for McDonald's personnel. Indeed, the data suggest that the impacts of this redesign of service delivery deploying people, devices, and networks in innovative configurations are dramatic. In one survey administered a year after a pilot call center went live, McDonald's found that average drive-thru order times had fallen by more than a minute. Friendliness of personnel as perceived by customers had risen by 11 percent. Order accuracy, the bugbear of the industry, was nearly perfect. (By some estimates, two-thirds of quick-serve orders placed in America are entered and/or fulfilled incorrectly.) And employee turnover, which can run as high as 240 percent annually, was reduced by half.[4]

It's hard to argue with results like these. The outcome is good for customers and good for employees, and it's good business for McDonald's; but it demands the radical redesign of service work, predicated on a decisively discontinuous model for how a firm can best manage its interactions with customers. For example, the call center plan, if it catches on, will increasingly move many front-line service employees (those engaged in information processing, such as order entry, electronic payment, expediting) out of the restaurants into call centers. Those call centers are located today in or near the local markets they serve. As scale economics come into play, though, some consumers may find themselves placing orders at local fast-food restaurants through their car windows talking with someone in India, Ireland, or the Philippines about the lunch they're about to consume. And those employees will never see or touch the food they're "serving."

The quick-serve industry, which employs several million people in the United States alone, is but one example of the radical redesign of service work that is unfolding. This front-office reengineering is driven by the proliferation of devices (from Web sites and kiosks to wireless headsets and handheld tablets) and the ubiquity of high-speed, low-cost networks (both wireline and wireless), and it's enabled by new approaches in deploying front-line service workers in the management of customer interactions. The call center configuration is but one example of a reengineered front office that presents a strikingly different picture of labor in the service industries. Underlying these developments is a nontrivial challenge facing managers in services today—how to determine the optimal division of service labor between people and machines.

THE CXO'S CHALLENGE

The CXO must determine both how to integrate the right interfaces into coherent systems to meet customer and company needs and how to deploy front-line people and machines within those interface systems to deliver an optimal division of labor. The CEO focuses broadly on a firm's strategic direction, but the CXO must design and manage the company's interface system to ensure that a company's optimal interface system becomes a reality and that, as a result, a firm goes to market with greatest effectiveness for customers and greatest efficiency for company operations. For most organizations, the very idea of such integration conjures up images of an unholy alliance of warring fiefdoms and silos, but that's precisely why the C-suite needs an individual with the power and authority to deliver integrated experiences for customers.

One case study, in particular, illustrates the points and themes made thus far. Bank of America represents an organization that has made the commitment to deliver outstanding customer experience by placing the management of all service interfaces under an individual executive, working in collaboration with the CEO, and functioning in a manner consistent with the role of a CXO.

Case Study—Ken Lewis and Liam McGee, Bank of America

Reengineering Bank of America's (BoA's) interfaces into a system that has achieved widespread admiration for its quality of service was no mean feat in the retail banking sector. According to ACSI, branch banking has among the lowest customer satisfaction ratings of any industry.[5] BoA has managed to buck the trend in many dramatic ways. As one of the largest retail banking companies in the United States, it has 33 million customer households in 29 states and the District of Columbia, along with international offices in 35 countries. It hosts 600 million customer visits annually in its branches, resulting in 1 billion face-to-face transactions with tellers and 1.1 billion transactions with ATMs. Its call centers field 700 million calls a year. On any given day, the bank processes 400 customer interactions a second.[6] Only an innovative combination of people and technology could enable the organization to serve, and serve profitably, a customer base of this kind. In this regard, CEO Ken Lewis and EVP Liam McGee have transformed the attitudes and behaviors of service personnel, aligning them with BoA's brand message, "Higher Standards," and have similarly enhanced BoA's many and various technology-mediated service interfaces. Last year, BoA's Web site came in first in customer experience ratings for retail banking consumers (according to Vividence) and, in the same period, ranked first among banking sites for small business (according to Gomez).[7]

The change process Lewis and McGee engineered began with a redefinition of BoA's branch banking business as a retail business. They recruited talent from retailers such as Home Depot, Wal-Mart, and The Gap, while adopting management lessons from Disney, ultimately measuring retail branch performance using the standard metric of the retail industry, same-store sales (for branches open one year), or "comps." They changed the incentives for retail associates, awarding them sales commissions for products and services that customers held beyond a period of four months, to ensure that selling was aligned with customer needs. They introduced a National Sales Management Playbook, with scripts that specified details of desired forms of customer interaction, including examples of the exact language tellers should use in greeting customers.[8]

Starting with the front-line service organization, Lewis and McGee translated the brand promise into employee attitudes and behaviors with something they called the "Bank of America Spirit." Involving coaching on what BoA viewed as "winning behaviors," the Spirit Program was designed to train front-line service personnel in the appropriate ways to interact with customers. In particular, Spirit placed an emphasis on the importance of making emotional connections with customers. It used performance concepts originated in the Disney theme parks, referring to "associates" as being "onstage" (facing customers) or "offstage" (on break) when on the job. When associates were onstage, they were expected to act proactively with customers, to smile and to show positive attitudes, and to embody responsiveness to customers' needs. When they were offstage or could otherwise not deliver on BoA's message of "Higher Standards," their training mandated that they withdraw from the service environment to an employee lounge, or remove their BoA name tags and other insignia identifying them as service personnel.[9] By focusing associates on a small number of simple service priorities that delivered on the brand message, BoA achieved a high degree of consistency across its branch banking network, including those branches it took over from Fleet Boston in a $47-billion acquisition of Fleet's operations.

To create an organizational context that supported this revitalized approach to service, BoA reorganized the bank around customer segments, not product lines or functional silos. Lewis, in particular, believed that the bank must drive customer satisfaction by using its array of service channels and interfaces both to listen to customers and to make it easier for them to get what they wanted. As Lewis observed, the key was "redesigning many of our sales and services processes with the customer at the center." He referred to the "formula": "Process improvement leads to greater customer satisfaction that leads to the customer doing more business with us that leads to revenue growth." Part and parcel of these changes was a focus on continuous improvement and productivity gains in operations, but getting there required linking people, technology, product lines, and functions together in an integrated system. As Lewis stated, "Our focus on process excellence includes improved ways for banking center associates to stay linked with their teammates in the mortgage, investment, and small business areas—as well as those in telephone banking, online banking, product development, and customer fulfillment—enabling them to give customers a more seamless, satisfying experience."[10] Tracking how well this complex system was serving customers depended on having a shared benchmark around which to rally the organization. The organization measured satisfaction on a 10-point scale, publicizing its success in achieving ratings only in the range of 9 to 10. Satisfaction at this level was what BoA called "Customer Delight." In the fourth quarter of 2001, the Customer Delight rating was 42.5 percent; three years later, in fourth quarter 2004, it had risen to 71 percent. (Each branch's performance was ultimately measured by McGee on a composite score with a 30-point scale.)[11]

In many respects, the most radical changes BoA made are visible to anyone who steps into its retail bank branches, which it reinvented as Banking Centers. Resembling retail environments much more than bank branches, the centers adopted open floor plans to engineer away the traditional barriers that separate bank personnel from customers. Each center had a "host station" just inside the entrance to greet and direct customers;

this was, in effect, a means to engage in service triage. Each center had advanced technology, starting with redesigned ATMs; accompanied by kiosks for accessing information about more complex products, paying bills, checking stock quotes, and printing statements; and automated systems for accessing safety deposit boxes using electronic palm scanners. In the back of each center, there were several tellers behind a service counter. Along the way, there were glass-enclosed meeting rooms for private customer conferences, and a lounge with comfortable seating, video monitors, and financial publications. Importantly, most associates spent their hours on the sales floor rather than behind counters, intercepting customers to address their needs proactively and pulling them out of lines when they could process their transactions elsewhere faster.

The process of optimizing the new store designs was continuous: BoA used what it called "voice of the customer" research to create more useful and welcoming environments at its centers, and it relied on an outside technology vendor, Brickstream, to capture center activity on video to explore ways to improve service. Some of the center improvements were not operational but psychological, identifying better ways to manage customer perceptions. For example, BoA found that it could reduce customer perceptions of wait times by at least 15 percent and as much as 26 percent by using what it called "distraction techniques." These included high-definition video displays with news or financial data in waiting areas as well as managers who greeted customers who were in line, helped some customers with selected transactions, and directed other customers to parts of the center where staff could address their needs more quickly.[12] To ensure that BoA was optimizing its blend of service delivered by people and machines, Lewis and McGee put in place metrics "to measure how a [new] technology affects service, customer satisfaction, brand staffing, and other factors, and tying the results into savings and profits."

Although most aspects of BoA's implementation were successful, the ultimate realization of the organizational transformation depended on the transition to a system-wide, back-end information system it called Model Bank, which would enable associates in any center nationwide to recognize a customer from any part of the system and to deal with any of BoA's many product lines. This common set of applications running on mainframes was the result of a 13-year effort and nearly $1 billion in custom development costs.[13] BoA had implemented it only on a regional basis, but the bank planned to make the transition from the acquired Fleet operations to the Model Bank platform in a move that represented the next major test.[14] At the same time, however, BoA's success deploying its online banking operation had attracted roughly half of the bank's checking account customers to bank online (as of April 2005, the online site had 13.2 million users).[15] Industry satisfaction rankings indicated that BoA's goal for the online site had been met. As one senior executive observed, it was "to ensure that customers who interact with us through the Web have a truly outstanding experience consistent with what they're used to in the branches."[16]

One ultimate measure of Lewis and McGee's success in orchestrating an interface system that truly works was the Fleet merger. Conventional wisdom suggested that banks merging retail operations generally lost 10 to 15 percent of their existing customers as a result of service disloca-tions. In the first three quarters after the merger, however, BoA actually added 174,000 new checking accounts in the former Fleet territory, versus 35,000 new checking accounts added in all of 2003, while eliminating nearly a billion dollars in costs.[17] That's arguably the outcome of man-aging a coherent, aligned, and integrated interface system to deliver service in ways that are brand-aligned, customer-satisfying, and loyalty-inducing, predicated on deploying people and machines in innovative ways. Performance for customers increased and costs to the company decreased—a truly felicitous combination of effects!

CONCLUSION

Unrealistic, you may say. Consider the alternatives. In our work, we find that even "best practice" companies deploy interface systems fraught with three basic forms of dysfunction: pain points, choke points, and drop-off points, which take their toll in reduced top-line growth, increased operating costs, or both.

Pain Points

Like the corporate Web sites previously referenced, interfaces that per-form poorly for customers drive dissatisfaction. Companies cannot "cre-ate" and "keep" customers without fixing human and machine interfaces to make them appealing, friendly, intuitive, and navigable. Generally, pain points are relatively straightforward to identify but complex to fix, because they involve crucial integration challenges. If left untended, they encourage customers to defect.

Choke Points

Companies may optimize individual interfaces, but success for cus-tomers depends on being able to move seamlessly through a system of interfaces to achieve a goal, such as a purchase transaction or service inter-action. The flow requires linkages or handoffs between interfaces within the system. Because choke points slow down or impede handoffs from one service platform to another, getting them right requires that disparate corporate operations must collaborate in seemingly "unnatural" ways to speed customers to their goals.

Drop-Off Points

Interfaces that prove sufficiently frustrating may drive customers away, and flawed linkages between interfaces may cause customers to flow less readily through an interface system. When such pain points or choke points become sufficiently serious, they become drop-off points—places where customers simply defect from the system. Mitigating drop-off points requires that managers use integrative approaches to deliver results across multiple corporate functions or departments; in some industries, it requires an extension of such coordination to entities, such as auto dealers, that brands orchestrating the experience neither own nor control.

Strategic issues such as these define the case for the CXO. Every organization must do what Bank of America did if it intends to compete at scale in the efficient and effective delivery of services. Interface systems have enormous strategic implications for firms, and they are fraught with operating complexities both financial and operational. Their orchestration cannot be left to chance. The job calls for leaders who can fluently speak the languages of human resources, operations, and technology, and who are deeply committed to understanding and to serving customers. They are the individuals who can lead workforces in innovative combinations with technology to reinvent how services are delivered. The appropriate caliber of leadership is at the C-level of corporations, but the challenges their management entails are too involved to depend on excess capacity in the CEO's schedule. Someone else must have the power and authority to design and operate interface systems that work, and that person is the CXO. She or he will hold the keys to their company's competitive future, and the time to source that person is now.

NOTES

1. Bruce D. Temkin, "Companies Deliver Subpar Customer Experiences," *Forrester Research*, January 7, 2005.

2. Bruce D. Temkin, "Customers Will Get More Attention in 2005," *Forrester Research*, January 10, 2005.

3. Bruce D. Temkin, "Who's in Charge of Customer Experience?" *Forrester Research*, December 27, 2004.

4. Barbara Kiviat, "Innovators: Forging the Future, Faster Food," *TIME*, April 4, 2005.

5. Daniel Cox and James Bossert, "Driving Organic Growth at Bank of America," *Quality Progress*, February 1, 2005.

6. Bank of America Web site, "Facts about the Corporation"; Bank of America, "Annual Report," 2004.

7. Ibid.

8. Dean Foust and Michael Eidam, "BofA's Happy Surprise," *BusinessWeek,* February 7, 2005.

9. Sasha Talcott, "Banking on Spirit," *The Boston Globe,* May 26, 2004.

10. Ken Lewis, "Sustaining Growth," Bank of America presentation, Credit Suisse First Boston Financial Services Conference, 8 February 2005, http://media.corporate-ir.net/media_files/NYS/BAC/presentations/csfb_020805.pdf (accessed May 24, 2005).

11. Bank of America, "Annual Report," 2004.

12. Stefan Thomke, "R&D Comes to Services: Bank of America's Pathbreaking Experiments," *Harvard Business Review,* April 1, 2003.

13. Mel Duvall, "Bank of America: Aiming Higher," *Baseline,* November 1, 2004 http://www.baselinemag.com/article2/0,1397,1720795,00.asp (accessed May 24, 2005).

14. Sasha Talcott, "Fleet Conversion to Be Big Test for Bank, *The Boston Globe,* May 24, 2005.

15. Bank of America Web site, "Online Banking Facts," http://www.bankofamerica.com/newsroom/presskits/pdfs/fastfacts.pdf (accessed June 8, 2005).

16. InQuira Web site, "In Search of a Better Banking Experience," December 2004, http://www.inquira.com/pdf/BofA_FS_Dec04.pdf (accessed May 24, 2005).

17. Jeremy Quittner, "B of A: 'Gradual' Fleet Merger Stems Attrition," *American Banker,* 170, 11, January 18, 2005, 16; Sasha Talcott, "Bank of America Making a Name for Itself," *The Boston Globe,* March 5, 2004; Constantine von Hoffman, "The Art (and Science) of the Deal," CMO, May 2005, http://www.cmomagazine.com/read/050105/art_science_deal.html.

CHAPTER 6

Products, Customers, and Front-Line Employees

Jay W. Lorsch

Here's fair warning: I'm coming at this topic as a consumer, not as a Professor at Harvard Business School. And to "cut to the chase" at the outset, I would urge all managers from the CEO to first-line supervisors to take the same perspective. Doing so is an easy way to take a quick leap forward in understanding your business and your employees.

You all shop. You all buy services. Ask yourself, when are you disappointed and when are you not? When do you come out of a store relaxed and feeling great about the experience and full of goodwill for the people you dealt with? When do you leave feeling disgruntled or even angry?

What about the services you receive from a customer representative over the phone or online? When do you end the conversation satisfied and when do you end it in frustration? What's the difference?

I've asked myself these questions, and I've also considered my knee-jerk reactions (as I've left stores or finished consultations with doctors, financial service experts, or whomever) in light of the prevailing theories on management. Here's what I've concluded.

The best way to improve the experience for your customers or clients is to tailor front-line employee training and measurement standards to customers' expectations based on the product or service your company is trying to sell. That is, start out by thinking about the product and the customer at the same time. Figure out what the customer needs and expects based on the product or service you want to deliver to her. Are you in a luxury shop, or a discount mall? Develop your policies and practices from there!

This may sound obvious and straightforward, and conceptually it is, but the question arises: if this is true, why don't more management teams think this way? I can only speculate about the answer to this question. My hunch is that there is a tendency to deal with matters relating to front-line employees in the manner that seems most cost effective. That is, management teams tend to hire those people who are most readily available, and use off-the-shelf training programs. They look at what others are doing and copy it whether or not it matches their situation. They don't "waste" precious management time analyzing their work situation and what it implies for motivating and developing these key employees.

Yet there's a lot to be gained from revisiting what should be "the basics" from this perspective. Start by thinking about products or services.

THE PRODUCT/SERVICE SPECTRUM

Consider Figure 6.1, "The Product/Service Spectrum." At the "simple" end of the spectrum you'll find products that people use regularly without any explanation or instructions: for example aspirin or dog biscuits, batteries. At the other end you'll see "knowledge." This refers to knowledge about more complex products or services, such as investments, medical treatments or prescriptions, or legal matters.

At the "simple" end are the many items that I select and buy without expectation of any input from the person I might encounter at the cash register. In fact I almost always pick them off the store shelf, stick them in a shopping cart or basket, and take them to the checkout counter myself. What's more, I usually buy several of these products at the same time in a store that may sell hundreds, if not thousands, of such items. Rarely do I have to consult an employee; rarely would I even entertain the thought that the employee might know anything more than I do about the product. I don't need to know anything about the innards of

Figure 6.1
The Product/Service Spectrum

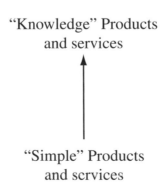

"Knowledge" Products
and services

"Simple" Products
and services

the battery, or what's in the dog biscuits. (Products in this category can actually be quite complex, but their complexity doesn't matter to the customer.) If I do want to know something about the product, I can usually find it on the label, in a brochure, or a Web site that the label will point me toward.

On those rare occasions when I want help from a front-line store employee, I don't expect much from them in terms of product knowledge, nor am I generally upset if they can't answer my question about the makeup or usage of a specific product. For example, I was recently in a large pharmacy (some readers would call it a "drug store") shopping for Gillette razor blades, of which there seemed to be a dizzying array. I asked the cashier which was the latest version, as I knew that this kind would fit my razor. I got a very confusing and uninformative response. In essence no help! But I wasn't bothered by this. In fact I expected it and was sympathetic. He couldn't be expected to know details of all the products in the store.

That's not to say that I do not want some things from the drugstore clerk, or similar employees in supermarkets, mini-marts, or discounters. I *do* want them to be able to tell me where the product is on the miles of shelves, and if it's not there when it will be back in stock. I may want to know if there is some special deal that will give me a discount, or if there will be such a deal soon, or if a new product will be on the shelves soon. I also want to feel that my transaction is being handled in an efficient and courteous manner. A smile and a simple thank you will usually do!

In a nutshell, when the products are simple in my mind, the level of service that will please me from a front-line employee is also simple.

Recognizing that there are many products and services in between the extremes, however, let's look at the other end of the spectrum, where the product or service is complicated. Many examples come to mind: automobiles, appliances, computers, and even fashionable clothing for both genders. Services such as medical treatment, financial planning, and legal advice are also at this end of the spectrum. Although there are obviously big differences between a legal consultation and buying an automobile, there are also similarities.

When I visit my lawyer, I am seeking advice, perhaps about tax matters or a real estate transaction. I am looking for knowledge about something with which I'm not familiar. I want my lawyer to explain things in a lucid and thorough manner. If he or she doesn't do this well, I shall leave dissatisfied, and if this happens too many times, I'm likely to seek a new attorney.

Buying a new car starts out differently, because I can see the new car and decide whether or not I like its appearance. I can also take it for a test spin and see whether I like its performance on the road. And of course I can read brochures about the car and check out its rating in auto magazines or on line. Yet in the end, especially if I'm considering purchasing a luxury car, say a BMW, Jaguar, or Mercedes Benz, I expect the car sales-person to help me in a fashion very similar to my lawyer. The salesperson not only needs to explain the financial aspects of the deal but also needs to be willing to explain why this car is preferable to competing products. Most important, as I get close to making an affirmative decision and espe-cially afterward, I expect the salesperson to be able to teach me how this computer on four wheels works! This may not require three years of law school, but it is a far cry from the stereotypical car salesperson of yester-year, whose only function was to make you believe he or she was giving you the best price possible.

At this end of the product/service spectrum, I expect other things. I want to be treated courteously by those who work for and with my prin-cipal contact. If someone makes an appointment with me, I expect it to be done efficiently, and that it will be kept without delay. I don't like sitting around law firm waiting rooms, any more than auto show rooms, even if they try to appease me with free coffee or soda. If I'm told documents will be sent to me for signature on a certain date, I expect them to show up with clear instructions about what I need to do. If I'm promised delivery of my new vehicle at a certain time, I don't want to be kept cooling my heels, while the salesperson finishes with a customer, who just walked in off the street. If I am about to spend tens of thousands of dollars, prompt and attentive service should go along with it.

Between these two ends of the product/service spectrum there are obvi-ously thousands of different products and services of varying degrees of complexity; however the basic point I have been making holds for each of them. If the product is simple, the level of service can be simple. If the product is complicated, the level of service needs to be of matching thor-oughness. Again, this sounds simple conceptually, but in practice this is not the case.

VARIATION IN CUSTOMER KNOWLEDGE

One source of difficulty is that consumers have varying degrees of knowledge about the product or service. I am a good example of this point when I am in a computer store. All around me are younger people who understand the technology much better than I. Whether they want to buy a new personal computer or a flat screen to augment their current setup, they are well informed. The help they need from the salesperson is simple compared to what I want. They may only want to know the fea-tures of competing products and the price, and they may have previously found much of this information online or from print advertising. Now I, and people like me, present a different problem for salespeople. We don't even know which questions to ask, or how to understand the advantages and disadvantages of various options. A salesperson can satisfy that informed customer in a few minutes, but he or she may have to spend a half hour or more with someone as uninformed as I. To satisfy me the salesperson not only has to know how to explain technical matters to a novice but also needs the patience of the proverbial Job!

Although such differences in customer sophistication are most apparent in the computer store, they exist in many other situations. This presents difficulties in determining what level of service and knowledge front-line employees should provide. If they are prepared to deal with customers like me, they need to be well trained and educated, a point I shall return to shortly. If they are prepared to deal with only knowledgeable customers, they'll find that customers like me will leave their store unhappy and frustrated. An obvious solution is to have front-line employees who can deal with both types of customers. Alternatively one could employee two types of employees: specialists for novices like me, and other salespeople for more informed customers. Either solution raises the cost of serving customers.

VARIATION IN CUSTOMER EXPECTATIONS

Closely related to variations in customer knowledge are variations in what customers expect and desire from front-line employees. For example, I occasionally accompany my wife on shopping expeditions for a new coat, dress, or suit. She is a person with a strong sense of taste. She feels she knows what fits her and what looks attractive when she wears it. When she goes into a shop or boutique, she wants to be left alone to look around and to browse through the racks. Any salesperson who approaches her and tries to convince her that something she has just past by will look good on her is certain to get a polite "brush off."

While my wife is doing her version of shopping, I usually find a comfortable chair near by so that I'm ready to offer my opinion, but only when asked. Meanwhile, as a longtime student of human behavior, I amuse myself by observing other women shopping. I find that some are similar to my wife and prefer to browse by themselves without much input from a salesperson. But I see many others walk directly up to the salesperson and ask for help. What's the latest fashion? Will this style look good on me? Have you got something in the stock room in a different color?

The challenge for the front-line personnel in this kind of scenario is to be sensitive to what the customer wants and expects. The wrong guess, especially if it is persistently pursued, can lead to a missed sale and an unhappy customer. In following my wife around on these shopping forays, I have seen experienced sales personnel approach her and immediately realize she doesn't want their active assistance. They quickly back off with, "Just let me know if I can be of assistance." They go off to do other things, while keeping a weather eye on my wife. Less astute personnel keep pressing, and the result, almost always, is that we quickly go to another shop.

So getting the right alignment between the product or service and the behavior of front-line personnel requires both an appropriate understanding of the customer's knowledge about the product and sensitivity to what level of service the customer desires. It is important to recognize that product knowledge and customer expectations are not always consistent. Sometimes customers who are not particularly knowledgeable about a product or service want to figure it out for themselves. Other customers who are quite sophisticated may still want to get their knowledge confirmed by the salesperson. Perhaps they just want to assure themselves that their knowledge is correct, or maybe they just want to demonstrate to the front-line employee that they know what they are talking about. Whatever the reason, the salesperson must be prepared to listen politely and respond accordingly.

THE COST OF CUSTOMER SERVICE

A third difficulty in aligning customer interactions and product complexity is the economics of getting it right. This is likely the most significant barrier to providing appropriate front-line service because of the intense competition among providers of services and products. Quite often a significant factor in this competition is the price at which the product or service is offered.

Take a simple product such as fast food. Many factors determine the appeal of one chain's offerings over others—store location, variety, taste—but the ability for the store and the company to compete and succeed financially often depends on the price of their food compared with that of competitors. Because the ultimate goal is profitability, low cost of food and of employees is an essential component in achieving the desired economic outcome. Fortunately, these businesses' customers have relatively low expectations of front-line employees. All they want is quick and accurate delivery of their meal at the desired price and quality.

This fact is well illustrated by a recent news story reporting that McDonald's was going to serve drive-thru customers at several locations from a central point. In essence, the customer places the order into a microphone communicating with the front-line employee miles away, who in turn sends the order back to the store at the point of purchase by computer. The savings for McDonald's is in the number of employees needed at drive-in windows. As long as the customer gets what he or she ordered promptly, the customer is a happy eater and McDonald's has reduced its costs.

Such an approach to serving customers is not limited to simple products. The world is full of service centers that provide more complicated customer service and sell more complex items. Airlines use them for reservations and flyer information. Automobile insurance companies use them to issue policies and to handle accident reports and claims. In some instances, like software support, the front-line employee may actually be half way around the world, perhaps in India.

All these efforts are intended to provide the appropriate level of service to customers at the least possible cost. For these products and services, the tactic seems to work. As we get to the more complex end of our spectrum, however, matters are different. For one thing, the economic issues are often different. For example, lawyers usually bill clients for the time they spend with them. Thus, they have an incentive to spend as much time as the client wants or needs. Other professional service providers may charge on a different basis: for investment advisors, a percentage of the assets under management; for doctors, a fixed fee for the visit or the procedure; for realtors, a percentage of the cost of the property. The precise metric used to determine the cost of the service varies among these professionals, but they all have some rough connection to the time required, as well as the value of the service to their client.

In most such services there is also another factor. Competitive success does not depend so heavily on the price of the service. Clients or patients are more concerned with the quality of the service, and if they believe it is superior they are willing to pay for it. Thus it is economically feasible for the service providers to deal with customers in a manner that is consistent with the complexity of the service, even though extra costs may be involved.

Economic issues can create constraints to providing the appropriate level of service in those situations where there is a complex product and intense economic competition. Two examples are personal computers and laptops, as well as automobiles. In both instances there is intense price competition among manufacturers and their dealers. Everyone on the selling side wants to get these products to the customer at the lowest possible cost. Yet, as I explained at the outset, many of these customers want a level of service from front-line employees that can be expensive. In my judgment, these situations are the most problematic.

But the challenge of aligning front-line behavior with the nature of the product or service is present all along the spectrum. In my experience the successful deployment of employees who interact with customers depends on achieving such a match.

IMPROVING FRONT-LINE SERVICE

The key to improving front-line service, then, is first to understand the nature of the product/service offering and the customers' needs in relation to it. With this understanding, it is possible to develop a human resource management system that can find, recruit, develop, and motivate front-line employees to serve customers in a manner that is consistent with what customers need and want, and the complexity of the product/service. For example, with simple products the focus should be on seeking employees who have the basic skills to handle check-out stations and to deal courteously with customers. Such employees also need training not only in the check-out process, but also in developing the basic knowledge to answer customer queries: Where do I find the toothpaste? When will you be getting in a shipment of this or that?

Of course, basic issues of fair treatment and adequate pay and benefits, as well as trust between these employees and their employer, matter and must be considered. But that's not the focus here. My message is that the true key to the success of front-line employees is aligning their behavior with the nature of their product and the needs of customers. This means finding and recruiting employees who have the appropriate knowledge and temperament. It means developing training programs and supervisory practices that encourage the relevant behavior. And it means using incentive practices that motivate the appropriate behavior. This will be more complicated than adopting off-the-shelf incentive programs or hiring the most available employment candidates. In my judgment, however, the extra effort and expense will pay off in satisfied customers and bottom-line results.

PART II

Riffs on the Here and Now

Susan was on the late shift at the fast-food restaurant. She had managerial experience with the company; in fact, she had been trained by the local franchise owner, but had taken time off after having a child and was now returning to the workforce part time. She wasn't a supervisor in this job; she had declined that opportunity. She just wanted to bring in some extra money.

At the end of her shift each evening, she meticulously cleaned the kitchen area, closing the business on schedule, but remaining to ensure that the place was ready for the next morning's shift. Her co-workers followed suit, and everything was going well, or so she thought.

A few weeks into her job, however, her supervisor called her aside and told her that she was going to be taken off the night shift. "You know that I can't work the other shifts," she reminded the supervisor. "If you take me off the night shift, I have to quit."

The supervisor said she was sorry, but that none of the other people on the night shift were willing to work with Susan any longer. They didn't want to work the extra time, the supervisor explained. It wasn't anything personal.

Susan was essentially forced to quit. As she says, looking back, "It really insulted me; the supervisor was trading down quality just to have enough bodies working, and she wasn't even willing to figure out a better solution."

What was going on at the front line in this situation? What kind of message was the front-line supervisor sending to the workforce? Where was the owner? How had Susan's training, received from the top, failed her at the front line? And what of the way the front-line jobs were designed?

Susan's story highlights some of the "disconnects" that occur as front-line employees do their work on a daily basis. Drilling down on the big picture, these next chapters offer advice for the "here and now" of front-line management.

CHAPTER 7

"We're Here to Help" (or Not)

Monica Higgins

Consider the following true story (the name of the employee has been changed, as has the name of the business):

It was Stacey's first Friday night working at Barney's Pizza. Her job was to take phone orders and counter orders, place them, and handle the food-money transactions with those customers. She had already worked the previous two nights, the first as a "shadow" to a more experienced staffer, the second by herself, and so she had some experience with the cash register.

By 6:30 P.M., the phone was already ringing steadily. It was much busier than the previous night. Stacey had taken a few orders correctly, both phone and counter, but on one phone order, she had neglected to ask if the customers wanted small subs or large. She had also neglected to clarify if their order of chicken tenders was the appetizer size, which is served "plain," or the dinner, which comes with fries.

When that customer arrived, she apologized profusely and clarified the order—small subs, appetizer tenders.

"No worries," the customer said. "I'm not in a rush."

Stacey then re-placed the order and started to ring it up, but she inadvertently began to ring in large subs rather than small. She caught her own mistake and said, "Oh wait, I'm sorry," but then as she started to void out the price of the large subs on the cash register, another waitress, walking by, pointed at the keyboard and said "You have to press this and then this to void it." Stacey nodded and started to proceed, but then as she extended her hand toward the keyboard, another waitress (evidently her supervisor), en route from a table back to the kitchen, said, "No, this one." The first waitress said, "That's what I told her, she has to go back."

"That's what I was going to do," Stacey said softly and tentatively raised her hand again to the keyboard, but the second waitress interrupted her action by saying, "this one, then that one," reaching over Stacey's hands to point.

A queue was forming behind the three women at the cash register, as another waitress waited with two orders to ring up. Meanwhile, the phone had begun to ring, and Stacey started to step back to answer it.

"I'll get it; you finish that," the first co-worker said. Stacey again turned to the cash register, and, with the second co-worker looking over her shoulder, pressed a button. She shot a nervous smile at the customer, who smiled back. She pressed another button, and then the first co-worker appeared again, waving an order ready to process. Stacey pressed a third button, and all three co-workers behind her shook their heads, reaching forward at the same time to correct what looked like another blunder. "That one," said one, pointing. Stacey went to press what she thought the co-worker had indicated. "No, That one."

It was clear that Stacey no longer had the faintest idea how to process the order. She looked at the cash register as if it she had never seen it before. She retreated, hands in the air, face red, eyes watering, as the supervisor took over, saying, "Don't worry; let me do it." Stacey, from the background, looked at the customer. "I'm sorry," she whispered.

What has happened here? We have a new front-line employee, who has been unfailingly polite to the customer. She has made an honest mistake, has acknowledged that mistake, and the customer is not unhappy.

We then have a possible stumble at the cash register and three more experienced staffers (one of them a supervisor) offering assistance.

None of them have been mean. The customer has been patient. But the more help Stacey gets, the less capable she becomes.

This type of scenario plays out frequently in many types of situations. When I heard the story, it reminded me immediately of an experience I had during the first year of my doctoral program. I remember freezing up at the computer when a senior professor asked me to do a statistical maneuver and then hovered over me, trying to help as I went through it. The more he tried to help, the clumsier I got. Later on, after a break, I was able to return to the project and complete it relatively easily. But the first time, the "helping" wasn't at all helpful.

When I recounted Stacey's experience to a colleague of mine, she immediately nodded in recognition as well. She remembers "the worst parallel parking job of my life," the time she was in a car with an off-duty driving instructor who was trying to give her pointers as she backed up. (This was years after she got her driver's license, and she swears that she never before or since has experienced that same level of difficulty in parking any vehicle.)

We've all "been there." At issue here, however, is how frequently the "Stacey Experience" is replicated at the front lines of work. Front-line employees are often trained, in large part, on the job; and many times, the trainee is put in the hot seat inadvertently by supervisors or co-workers who are only trying to help.

Helping, in these cases, isn't helpful. In fact, it has the exact opposite effect.

Clearly, many front-line employees need help on the job, especially early on. And clearly, it is the responsibility of the manager to provide that help when it is needed. So what is a manager to do? How can he or she ensure that the help being offered is actually helpful?

THREE CONSIDERATIONS

Years ago, I conducted a lab study to find out more about when "helping is helpful" and when it isn't. The study was conducted outside the realm of business. In fact, it centered on people trying to learn how to play a game involving mini-basketballs and a wall-mounted net with a chute to return the balls back to the player, regardless of whether they made a basket. I offer the broad findings here in the interests of floating ideas to jumpstart or prompt new thinking about front-line employees' effectiveness and experiences.[1]

After an initial "introduction" to the task, in which a third party demonstrated the game and explained the rules, participants were allowed to begin. The third party observer then either (1) did nothing but watch, (2) stepped in during the first round of play to offer "help" (much the way Stacey was helped), or (3) offered help after the first round of the game, during a subsequent round of play.

For some participants' experience, the third party was billed simply as a friendly observer, there to provide assistance. For others, the third party was billed as an evaluator, whose job it was to keep track of performance.

The results of the study suggested that there are several critical factors to consider when offering help to someone who is trying to learn a new task: (1) whether the person offering the help is perceived as an evaluator, or judge, of performance, (2) the level of confidence in the person who is learning the task, and (3) the timing of the help.

Perhaps not surprisingly, the study participants who were not being "evaluated" improved their skills more quickly than those who were being evaluated. These findings complemented much published research. Social psychologists have suggested that expectations of evaluation can negatively affect individual-level performance on vigilance tasks[2] and creative tasks[3]. They have also demonstrated that it is evaluation by an "other" (such as a supervisor), rather than evaluation by oneself, that results in poor performance of a task.

Study participants who exhibited more initial confidence also improved their skills more rapidly than their apparently less-confident peers.

The timing issue was more complicated in that participants tended to react differently to help offered at a given time depending on their perception of the person doing the advising.

When the "learners" were helped during their first attempt at the task by an "evaluator," they tended not to improve rapidly, or to freeze up, much as I did when I was trying to run that statistical maneuver in front of my professor. Early help like that, the study suggested, is construed as being corrective help. It implies that the person attempting the task at hand is deficient in some way and would not be able to perform the task without help. Such negative expectations of outcomes fuels the learner's motivation to protect himself or herself, and so leads one to try to shift attention away from the task at hand. Doing so, however, undermines the learner's ability to benefit from the help.

When the help was offered early on by the third-party-as-friendly-observer, recipients were better able to improve their performance. Learners seemed to understand that the third party was stepping in as a result of a personal concern to help the individual learn, rather than to form an evaluation.

Help given in a subsequent round of the game by a "friendly third party," the study suggested, was also perceived as being "helpful" and the participants were receptive and able to put the advice or assistance to good use. Help given later by an evaluator, on the other hand, was not received or processed as well; negative feedback such as this is hard to process when you are in learning mode. Again, when the environment was "friendly" and focused on learning, participants improved more rapidly than when the environment was "evaluative" or focused on performance.[4]

FROM PAGE TO PRACTICE

Although I'd be hard pressed to draw a direct connection between my study and Stacey's experience, the results, coupled with research on learning and performance, suggest several specific areas managers might consider when trying to improve the front-line employee experience and help employees contribute more fully to the company.

Chief among those would be the dual nature of the front-line supervisor's job. In 1997, Harvard Business School Professor Mike Beer wrote a powerful article, "Conducting a Performance Appraisal Interview."[5] In it, he explored why "performance appraisals" often do more to damage an employee's performance than foster improvement.

Managers, he noted, are simultaneously (1) trying to help employees develop (which requires counseling, coaching, career planning, and an open dialogue with employees) and (2) seeking information from or about individuals on which to base rewards or make personnel decisions (which by nature are evaluative and can cause employees to be defensive, put them "on their guard" or, simply, make them nervous).

The manager's role as "coach" or "developer of talent" can conflict directly with his or her equally important role as the person who evaluates employees on behalf of the company, and who deploys human resources based on performance.

And unless the manager fully understands that conflict, and takes steps to decouple the two roles, the employee can't benefit fully from a performance appraisal.

Similarly, even when no formal appraisal is underway, employees may find it difficult to accept or process "help" unless the supervisor is somehow able to communicate that the help is being offered in support, rather than judgment.

Decoupling these two roles is hard to accomplish in any scenario, but my sense is that it is extremely difficult at the front lines of work, especially in situations where the business model calls for a supervisor to monitor and measure quality, and allows little time for a low-stress learning curve.

I suspect that decoupling the manager's role is also particularly difficult at the front lines of work because the managers themselves are often "first timers." They're experiencing the dual nature of their roles as evaluators and coaches for the first time; they're also exploring the unfamiliar territory of being a leader and a subordinate simultaneously, and of having to build their own team while finding their place in the greater network of the organization. This can be particularly difficult when that "network" exists largely in remote locations, and is accessible mostly over the phone or computer. It can also be difficult when the "network," such as it is, is breathing down the manager's neck. Think back to Stacey. Her supervisor's manager (in the form of the pizza shop's owner) was watching it all happen from behind a bar on the other side of the room. Strains of the same conflicting themes were no doubt playing out for the supervisor as well. No pressure there!

What this might suggest to a company trying to bolster the front lines? For large and small companies, devoting more time and effort to the development of front-line managers might be a place to start. However, keep these three points in mind:

1. The *lesson* for managers to learn appears to be relatively simple: it is important to ensure that employees can make the distinction between when helping is just helping, and when performance is being evaluated.

2. The manager's *delivery* of the lesson might also be fairly uncomplicated. A manager might, for example, preface an attempt to "help" by commenting: "No grades being given today;" or "Just trying to help you get the hang of things;" or "Don't worry, it's a lot to learn on-the-job; we've all been there;"

or some such thing. This decreases the employee's perception that he or she is being evaluated and may, in fact, increase his or her confidence and motivation to try harder. The manager might also be clear about limiting performance appraisals to evaluation and discussing career-development and personal goals separately. (Michael Beer's article, *"Conducting a Performance Appraisal Interview,"* is an excellent guide to this process.)[6]

3. But *ingraining a habit or a behavior* that "sticks" amid the daily grind of customer service, meeting numbers, and other pressures is difficult and requires substantive effort up front (in the form of education and training) and in real time (in the form of reinforcement from managers up the line, and goals and incentives that complement the desired behavior). That's where something that seems so simple in concept (once its understood) falls apart in execution.

Linda Hill, a professor at the Harvard Business School, has conducted extensive research on new managers. Consider the following short passage from an article about her work:

To encourage the kinds of developmental relationships essential for new managers to succeed, companies must establish a culture characterized by a strong coaching orientation.

"Unfortunately," Hill notes, "many companies don't value managerial development—they have more of a 'sink or swim' mentality."

This is especially the case, says Hill, when economic times are tough: people become fare more focused on their company's current financial performance, and learning and development fall by the wayside. And when the economy's in trouble, it's much harder to create an environment of psychological safety within which people can make and learn from mistakes and feel comfortable asking for help.

Companies must always make tradeoffs between current performance and long-term learning. In Hill's experience, the few firms that do value development tend to focus educational efforts on their more senior managers and executives.[7]

Why not invest more deeply in front-line employees and in their managers? It's true that these employees do not set strategic direction, manage divisions, or run company-wide functions. But they meet the customer face-to face every day; it's their impact, coupled with the quality of the product itself, that impresses (or depresses!) the customer.

Stacey, by the way, has gained confidence at the cash register, and three months into her job, she gives every impression of being completely confident in her ability to tackle the tasks at hand. With one exception. Whenever the customer who witnessed that first Friday night snafu shows up at the counter, Stacy invariably makes a mistake at the cash register and has to void out the order and start again. She's clearly psyched out, even though the customer is unfailingly patient and polite. But that's a puzzle for another day.

NOTES

1. For details about the study, see Monica Higgins, "When Is Helping Helpful? Effects of Evaluation and Intervention Timing on Basketball Performance," *The Journal of Applied Behavioral Science* 37, 3 (September 2001): 280–298, NTL Institute; see also, J.M. Harackiewicz, S. Abrahams, and R. Wageman, "Performance Evaluation and Intrinsic Motivation: The Effects of Evaluative Focus, Rewards, and Achievement Orientations," *Journal of Personality and Social Psychology* 53 (1987): 1015–1023.

2. S.G. Harkins and I. Zysmanski, "Social Loafing and Self-Evaluation with an Objective Standard," *Journal of Experimental Social Psychology* 24 (1988): 1214–1229.

3. T.M. Amabile, "Effects of External Evaluation on Artistic Creativity," *Journal of Personality and Social Psychology* 37 (1979): 221–233.

4. Higgins, "When Is Helping Helpful?" 280–298; see also Harackiewicz, Abrahams, and Wageman, "Performance Evaluation and Intrinsic Motivation," 1015–1023.

5. "Conducting a Performance Appraisal," January 30, 1997, a "note" prepared by Professor Michael Beer as a basis for classroom discussion; copyright © 1997 by the President and Fellows of Harvard College.

6. Ibid.

7. *Harvard Management Update* article reprint number UO309E, "Debriefing Linda A. Hill," by Lauren Keller Johnson; see also *Harvard Management Update* article reprint number U9707C, "What You Must Learn to Become a Manager: An Interview with Linda Hill," and Linda A. Hill, *Becoming a Manager* (Cambridge: Harvard Business School Press, 1992).

CHAPTER 8

The Seven Deadly Sins of Corporate Miscommunication

Sam I. Hill and Rachel E. Hill

In the mid-1970s, one of the authors of this chapter spent two years in a remote village in Sierra Leone as a Peace Corps volunteer. At the time, the attrition rate for volunteers in West Africa was unacceptably high. The underlying drivers were complex and varied, but one of the most perplexing was a phenomenon called "rejection," which is exactly what it sounds like; the host village simply decides it doesn't like having the volunteer around and creates an environment in which he or she leaves.

Conventional wisdom explained rejection like this: those volunteers who did not master the local language were less able to communicate with their neighbors, integrated less quickly and thoroughly, and thus were more prone to rejection. A good hypothesis, but unfortunately, studies found it to be only half right. The happiest and most productive volunteers were indeed those who communicated well with the people in their villages, but it had nothing to do with language skills. In fact, some of the best-integrated volunteers actually relied on crude hand signals and mispronounced nouns to get their points across. And some of the least successful spoke one or more of the 15 local languages fluently.

The key to understanding this apparent inconsistency is to understand the village environment. Meryl Streep doesn't need words to communicate, and neither do volunteers. A tall, blond American stands out among 200 short, black people. Volunteers are watched continuously, 24 hours a day. Every move and expression are carefully noted and studied. The villagers always knew what they meant, whether or not they knew what the volunteers said. If the volunteer *meant* impatience or intolerance or insincerity, the word spread quickly, and the village simply turned its collective back.

In the corporate village, management gets the same scrutiny to the same result. Every smile in the cafeteria, rolling of the eyes at a company meeting, frown during a budget review, and sigh on the elevator are noted and passed along. Every perk (or perk removed) and sudden change in daily schedule convey information and are absorbed and acted on by the organization. In every corporation, those in management communicate continuously and effectively, even when they don't say a word.

Front-line employees pick up on this natural communication, and it affects them, often far more than more "official" or formal communications. That snarl on the disgruntled flight attendant's face when a passenger asks for a coffee refill is a perfect replica of his supervisor's expression at the morning briefing, and that smile and handshake from the store greeter are an exact copy of the ones she got yesterday from the visiting regional manager. Neither communication came via the company e-zine, but both were communicated loud and clear.

WHAT NOT TO COMMUNICATE

There are seven things a manager *never wants* to communicate to his or her front line, formally or informally, verbally or with body language. Call them the seven deadly sins of corporate miscommunication: (1) greed, (2) dishonesty, (3) laziness, (4) complacency, (5) rudeness, (6) hypocrisy, and (7) disdain for process.

Greed

In the 1987 movie *Wall Street*, a character named Gordon Gecko struts down the center aisle of a classroom and defiantly proclaims, "Greed is good." Many managers aren't quite so blunt, but they manage to get the same point across—always talking in employee meetings about stock price, laying on the corporate perks, and constantly discussing their personal wealth with anyone who will listen. (It is strange and a little bit sad to hear a CEO worth eight figures complain about his compensation compared to his peers while a minimum-wage janitor stands two feet away. But it is not uncommon.)

On the surface, using greed as a motivator sounds like an idea soundly rooted in human psychology. It taps into a basic stimulus, and outsized rewards get people's attention disproportionately; watch the interest in lotteries increase when the potential pay-outs reach $20 million. Therefore, what's wrong with using greed to align and propel organizational behaviors? It certainly appears to have worked for some companies. Investment banks, management consultancies, and law firms use the ostentatious and opulent lifestyles of the senior partners to incent younger staff to extreme personal sacrifices. Many a start-up has used the promise of huge riches to lure top-tier talent away from plush corner offices in New York to garages in Palo Alto.

The problem is, greed rarely works for the front line, and even when it does, it has very costly side effects. For example, truly large financial payouts are, with very rare exception, unrealistic for all but a handful of employees in a handful of companies. Think Microsoft. It is absolutely impossible for a sizable company to honestly promise wealth to front-line employees. The CEO may think that posting stock charts in the supermarket lunchrooms encourages checkout clerks to work harder, but not so. Those clerks are poor; they 're not dumb. They know that whatever Alan Greenspan does this morning has a lot more to do with the direction of that squiggly line than what each of them does. Sure, if the stock goes up, that's great. But there's many a job change and pink slip twixt that chart and retirement, and stock appreciation is not going to buy their kids' new school clothes.

There is an even bigger problem with using greed to motivate. It has terrible side effects. It creates a rift between the boastful wealthy and the seething, envious rank and file. Take American Airlines, who in 2003 secured almost $2 billion in concessions from the unions of their mechanics, pilots, and flight attendants to help the airline avoid bankruptcy. They had simultaneously set up a trust for executives' pensions to protect them in case of bankruptcy and promised executives bonuses of up to twice their salary for staying with American until 2005, which (discovered only 24 hours after the unions had agreed to cuts) prompted outrage from the rest of their employees.[1]

But most dangerously, greed is a treadmill. A lot is never enough. Macro-greed encourages micro-greed, and micro-greed can easily spill over into chiseling hours on timesheets, stealing staplers, and a thousand other petty, but cumulatively damaging behaviors.

Dishonesty

No organization boasts about being dishonest or having no integrity. (Even the mob thinks of itself as composed of men of honor.) But many organizations are. Employees hide broken cases on the back of the pallet. Call center operators fib to get the order. Supervisors fabricate data for reports. Salespeople put their thumb over the disclaimer on the warranty as the customer signs the contract. And sooner or later, institutional dishonesty morphs into individual dishonesty. Employees pilfer tools, ring up groceries at a lower price for friends, or use company cars for personal use. It's all dishonesty, institutional or individual, and it gets communicated from the top.

For example, almost every sales force has some version of the "hat" story, about a young salesman who, forced to buy a hat by his boss, puts it on his expense account and has the charge disallowed, only to submit a revised report for the same bottom-line amount (but no hat) with a note clipped to the top of the page which reads "Find the hat!" It's a funny story, but like all corporate fables, it is intended to send a message. In this case, the message is clear: Don't let honesty get in the way of results. And don't get caught. That's bad managing and bad thinking.

Laziness

Laziness is the deep, dark secret of corporate America. Many companies struggle because their employees don't work very hard, and employees don't work very hard because their leaders discourage them from doing so.

That may sound anachronistic, a throw-back to the days of sweatshops and 12-hour factory shifts. Not really. Over the last few decades, we have worked for, visited, and studied hundreds of companies. On average, what stands out at better companies is that employees work hard *and* smart. Wal-Mart store managers arise before dawn and Pepsi drivers move on a dead run. An Alamo desk clerk rarely makes you wait until he finishes that magazine article on Britney. There are reasons good organizations succeed and one reason is they work at it.

To be fair, like dishonesty, no company thinks of itself as lazy. No manager has ever stood up in an employee meeting and said "Laziness is good" or issued a memo that says "Let's become as productive as Europe." In fact, just the opposite—at every company we visit, top managers spend hours telling us how overworked their employees are and assert that 55-hour weeks are the norm. (It's never true, by the way. Measured workweeks are far shorter and the amount of personal time taken at work is significant. The lazier the company, the longer the reported workweek.)

So how have managers communicated that laziness is OK? It happens in many ways. If front-line employees see their managers usurp the work day for corporate play, for example, golf outings and ropes courses, that sends a pretty clear message. And look at the executive offices. If offices are filled with Nerf balls or golf trophies rather than competitor advertisements, stacks of data, or new products, that sends a message that the first priority of the company is fun and games, and the second (or third or fourth) is hard work. But, of course, the most powerful of all communications is by example. If managers don't work hard, front-line employees won't either. At the Mexican super-company, Cemex, senior managers are discouraged from playing golf because golf playing occurs on Saturday, when many of their drivers and warehouse people are working.

Understand, we're not suggesting that companies abuse employees by cheating on overtime or taking short cuts on safety or health. We're just suggesting that people should work hard when they're at work. But what about overwork? Over time won't that damage a company by leading to work errors, turnover and burnout? Isn't there an equal danger of creating an environment of extreme hours and face time for face time's sake? No.

Complacency

We have long been tempted to create a measure to predict impending corporate crises. We'd call it the Smug Index, a qualitative evaluation of how complacent companies are based on conversations with their employees. Complacency occurs at every level.

- On the list would be the Australian food company whose CEO laughed off poor performance by explaining that the company's ownership structure made it "take-over proof." Two weeks later, to the day, his company was taken over in a hostile bid and he was retired.

- Add to the list the airline employee who told us that it didn't matter if we didn't like his airline, because there are only two that matter at O'Hare, and if we walked away from his counter, sooner or later we'll get mad with the other airline and come crawling back.

Complacency is an almost inescapable by-product of success. It is particularly prevalent in employees who joined after the company had already gained recognition for its accomplishments and built a marble corporate headquarters. Complacency is a naturally occurring function, and, as such, it takes very little encouragement for it to grow. The mandate, therefore, is for managers not to do anything by word or deed that accelerates it.

What's on the list of things not to do? First is being dismissive or relaxed about new competitors or new threats. At Wal-Mart store meetings, managers continually warn employees about all the companies that are coming after them. To hear Wal-Mart tell it, every competitor is positioned to drive it into the ground if it relaxes for a split second. It's not terribly accurate, but it discourages complacency.

Second is accepting excuses for underperformance. Two years ago at Frito Lay, a recently recruited manager walked into his boss's office and requested that the manager call headquarters and tell them that as a result of aggressive competitor pricing cuts, the unit would miss their budget. The boss shoved the phone across the table and said, "I need this job. You call, and when you do, tell them I have no intention of missing plan," and walked out of the office.

Finally, there is a vocabulary of complacency. There are obvious terms like *unchallenged market leader*. But there are also more subtle phrases such as *natural cost escalation, using our pricing power, waiting for competitors to come to their senses"* and *recognize we're in a mature market.* Anything that signals a willingness to accept the status quo rather than being relentlessly driven toward improvement is a clear signal for complacency.

And for the record, we know there are only two major airlines at O'Hare. But one of them gets 90 percent of our firm's business. We haven't come crawling back yet, and we don't plan to.

Rudeness

One of the great myths of popular culture is that we are becoming a ruder society. We studied this "trend" for an earlier book and found that it is an evergreen complaint—every generation feels the generation that follows it is ruder than its own. This occurs because standards of politeness are continually changing, for example, the "N" word is now out, the "F" word is now semi-acceptable. Still, whatever their definition, people dislike rudeness, are offended by it, and remember it.

We will never forget the Northwestern gate agent who, when asked (politely) to change a seat on a flight, tossed the ticket jacket back across the podium and snapped, "You bought seats, you got seats, now get on the plane." With hundreds of flights on Northwestern between us, we must assume that there have been innumerable instances of politeness by their front-line staff, not one of which we remember. But we do remember that guy.

Avoiding rudeness is important for front-line staff for two reasons. The first, obvious reason is that to the customer in front of the podium, the gate agent *is* Northwestern Airlines. A second, and more subtle reason, is that modern service organizations have rudeness built into them already, and front-line staff must be excessively polite just to keep the rudeness meter at neutral. To revisit the earlier example, it is very likely the flight was oversold and there were no available alternate seats. Therefore, we were going to be offended anyway because the seats we'd reserved were not available. The agent piled personal rudeness on top of systemic rudeness.

It is hard for front-line staff not to be rude to customers, because customers are often jerks. Our feet hurt from Christmas shopping, the kids started screaming for a McFlurry 200 miles ago in Wichita, and this is the fourth flight this week. We're tired and cranky and frustrated with the inflexibility of dealing with mammoth service factories, and so we say things to front-line staff we would never say to service staff we know, like the postman or the cleaning lady. To handle this onslaught, front-line staff need the patience of Mother Theresa and the stoicism of the guardsman in front of Buckingham Palace. Most don't have it. (We don't have it either.)

But managers can exacerbate this customer characteristic inadvertently. Some companies attempt to have two standards of politeness: one internal and one external. That is, internally managers are nasty to employees, but they then plaster a smile on when a customer wanders within earshot. It's asking too much of front-line staff to ask them to maintain and selectively apply two inconsistent standards of behavior. Invariably internal rudeness shows through.

Another way that managers signal that rudeness is acceptable is by direct example. When a supervisor fires back at an abusive customer, she may think she's doing the right thing by sticking up for her abused staff and engendering loyalty. In reality, she's sending a message that politeness is situational and a judgment call. Not a good idea.

Hypocrisy

Hypocrisy—parents do it, kids do it, celebrities and politicians and the media do it, employees and managers alike do it. We do it. You do it. Saying one thing and doing another is part and parcel of our daily lives, a way of smudging over the many conflicting objectives we all have. It can't a big deal, right? Wrong.

Hypocrisy breeds mistrust of superiors, creates an atmosphere that fosters deception, and perhaps worst of all creates confusion and indecision in the front line. Imagine you're a clerk in a furniture store and at the morning meeting, your manager tells you that declining sales mean everyone has to hustle, or she'll be forced to cut hours. She then spends the majority of the day in the back office playing computer solitaire and infrequently fielding calls. You can't call her on it—she's your boss. But you can carp to your co-workers. You might steal an extra 10 minutes on your lunch break because your feet are killing you, justifying it because she sits down all day. And when that opportunity comes for a big sale, how hard do you press to close it, to cross-sell, up-sell, accessorize? If the situation was really that dire, wouldn't she be on the sales floor, too?

Managers encourage a "do what I say, not what I do" culture by setting rules for which they themselves show little regard. When the boss hands out a 100-page document to the sales force, calls a meeting to discuss it, and asks his assistant to summarize it instead of reading it himself, the message is clearly sent that it's not that important.

If an organization wants to be more customer-friendly, and the managers make fun of a customer behind his back, you can bet that people are going to take notice. Especially if they're doing it right next to that giant motivational poster that says "The Customer Comes First." Better a manager that eschews motivation altogether than one who says one thing and does another.

Disdain for Process

The other afternoon we checked in a car at the Pittsburgh airport. When the young attendant handed us our receipt, we looked at it and asked her if she'd heard us say we didn't refuel. "Yeah, I gave you a break on the gas," she replied with a smile. Surprised, we awkwardly thanked her and ran for our flight. We'd just encountered the monster that lurks under every line manager's bed: someone who ignores process.

Don't get us wrong. We're not process junkies. We know that an obsession with process can lead to stultification and decay, as occurred, for example, at McDonald's.

But there's a place for process, and the front line is such a place. Look at Home Depot, the second largest retailer in America. When Bob Nardelli arrived in 2000, the company was smug, confident, and fiercely proud of its independent no-process culture. But soon after he took over, the company began to stumble under pressure from rival Lowe's, and the stock price began to slide. General Electric alum Nardelli decided it was time for process and instituted a broad-ranging program of process definition, training, and measurement. It has worked. Home Depot's growth has taken off again, and even old-timers who remember the rock 'n' roll days agree it's a much better company today than it was five years ago.

Nardelli chose to inculcate process discipline by introducing a high-profile program called Six Sigma. Six Sigma programs have become very popular, not only because they give process discipline a name, but also because they signal to organizations that process discipline is for everyone, from the top to the front line. Regardless of whether a company decides to formally introduce a comprehensive process program, every company should be careful not to undermine process. Pre-Nardelli, store managers at Home Depot used to make a big show of tearing up memos from the head office. Many of those same managers still got promoted. It's hard to send a clearer signal than that to the 300,000 shop assistants that conformity to process is not a priority.

Disdain for process is particularly lethal in the front line. The rental car company in Pittsburgh probably won't miss the $8 we owe them, but they sure as heck will if that same behavior is multiplied by 30 employees each at 1,500 locations for 365 days a year.

LETHAL, BUT EASY

That's it, our seven deadly sins of corporate miscommunication: (1) greed, (2) dishonesty, (3) laziness, (4) complacency, (5) rudeness, (6) hypocrisy, and (7) disdain for process. They're lethal, they destroy great companies, and they're surprisingly easy to communicate. And it doesn't really matter what language you use. Or don't use.

NOTE

1. Edward Wong, "American's Executive Packages Draw Fire," *New York Times*, April 8, 2003.

CHAPTER 9

No Time to Be Authentic?

Ton Plekkenpol

After the commodities economy came the product economy. After the product economy came the service economy. Now we have arrived at a perception economy. This economy encompasses products and services, but today, we can also name, brand, and market the chemistry between companies and their customers.

In fact, we should. Customers are increasingly firm about the standard of product quality they expect; they're increasingly firm about the minimum service standards they'll tolerate. But it seems as if they are still surprised and pleased when a genuine connection is made between company and consumer, between front-line employee and the person that employee is helping.

Therein lies an opportunity. But few companies are truly positioned to take advantage of it.

Here are the problems.

First, many companies we know still rely on static, dated approaches to educate their own employees about their brands. They teach these employees to interact with customers using heavily scripted speech, which naturally results in a stilted conversation between seller and buyer, if it results in any conversation at all. All too infrequently are considerations for feeling and mood blended into the way in which salespeople and the companies they represent present themselves. This despite all the talk about the importance of the customer's "experience." The fact is, in this regard, many managers sense and even know what's needed, but they lack the tools or know-how to teach staff members how to deliver.

Second, customers seek authenticity in their relationships with sales-people and other front-line employees, and most companies don't truly understand what "authenticity" means, much less how to provide it. In fact, companies pursuing delivery of a particular customer "experi-ence" often do so at the expense of authenticity and would be better off not even making the attempt. There is a misunderstanding on the part of most companies about what authenticity can mean to a customer. Training front-line employees to say "havaniceday" to each customer in turn isn't it. Training front-line employees to say "howareyoudoing" also isn't it. And "HowmayIhelpyou" works only if the follow-up, in response to the customer's answer, is satisfactory. Authenticity means engaging with the customer in a genuine way, if time permits. Authenticity also means choosing not to engage if the transaction time doesn't allow for it.

How can companies overcome these two problems? First, managers need to identify and understand how front-line employees represent the company's brand, and what, in fact, that role means in terms of employee behavior with customers.

Second, they need to understand the front-line employee experience well enough to prescribe solutions that will translate effectively to the front lines. Mandating that employees ask customers a certain question during each interaction, or make a certain promotional offer, will not get at the authenticity and experience customers seek if those questions or offers are delivered under pressure. One has only to buy a coffee at a very busy time of day in certain chain locations to see this problem exemplified. The front-line employee is under extreme pressure to deliver the product and service as required. The authenticity of the purchase "experience"— and the personification of the brand—cannot be enhanced by requiring that same highly stressed employee to feign the ability to make small talk with genuine interest at the same time.

Ironically, one of the best ways to help top managers—and front-line employees—best understand how they function as a part of the brand, and also how they can provide authentic support in that position, is to role-play.

We have recently worked with Nortel, a telecommunications company. One of the issues we've helped the company address is how to raise its technical engineers' awareness regarding their role as ambassadors of the company. These engineers talk with customers all the time on the help line; their jobs provide a critical link with customers, and yet when we started our work, most if not all of the company's "techs" were utterly unaware of their potential to influence customers and reflect on the company's brand.

A simple explanation of the potential of their role would not have sufficed. A mandate from top managers to "promote" a certain product or service or to "engage" the customer regarding new product developments would not have sufficed. Not only would these directives have stayed on the printed page, but also this approach would have inadvertently supported a notion that top managers didn't understand the nature and scope of what a technical employee has to get done to fulfill his or her basic job responsibilities. It would have seemed like an "extra" expectation, and one that might have sounded "nice" but had no grip on reality.

Instead, we took the company's vision of itself and its brand and used it as a point of departure to dramatize what the brand represented in a technical employee/customer interaction, and what bearing that type of robust interaction has on the employee's job design, needed tools, support, and so forth.

People in organizations often cooperate without feeling good about or actually being involved with passion in what they are doing. Role-playing customer scenarios with managers at all levels and with front-line employees, and then considering what is learned against the backdrop of the employees' actual jobs can help bridge that gap.

IS THE STRUCTURE SUPPORTIVE?

Another way to make significant progress in engaging front-line employees as brand representatives, as well as enhancing top managers' understanding of what front-line employees need to deliver the authenticity customers seek, is to reconsider the company's formal communications plans and infrastructure.

Traditionally, many companies developed separate internal and external communication plans. Internal plans deal with how information was passed from managers to managers to employees. External plans deal with appointed "spokespersons," who deal with the media and with the community. In addition, there would likely be a "human resources plan," concerning training and development, which was managed by a representative of Human Resources (HR), or "personnel."

There was seldom any integration between these disciplines. And even when connections could be made, or recognized, the plans were implemented separately. It is time to integrate all of these communication plans and policies. It is time to overhaul how information is moved internally and externally, to eliminate overlap, and to create unified, company-wide communications systems.

Companies, of course, need formal media liaisons and clear limits regarding formal statements made to the media or the community. We are not suggesting otherwise; however, we are suggesting that it is time to recognize explicitly that all front-line employees are company spokespeople. Their job design should incorporate that understanding, and their training and development should reflect it. We are also suggesting that having separate trajectories of knowledge within organizations is increasingly a waste of time and money. The HR department is a good place to begin the unification process. The Communications department is another. Put their heads together; marry people development with job design and knowledge-sharing and manager/employee communications. Watch printed maxims leap off the page.

Knowledge must be visualized and at the same time dramatized. It needs a personality that touches employees and managers alike. Once a company has identified that personality, it is so much closer to being able to turn an aggregate of people into a business. If, internally, we can touch that emotion and that inspiration in a dramatic way that makes us feel what it is we actually signify as a group, it then becomes easier to capture the essence in an external communication plan.

Practically, the people working on and with that external plan then have an edge when it comes to conceiving of budget-friendly, PR-building activities that attract and motivate customers. What's easier to understand is easier to define and convey.

Consider again our technical engineers at Nortel. One of the critical inputs to their dramatic exercise was the requirement that they translate their existing vision into a role-playing scenario *themselves.* By having to think up the presentation themselves, they in fact also learned how many different ways they could communicate with customers and clients. In this way, they were able to learn how they could actually be representative ambassadors. They learned to spot the opportunities to suggest products or services that came about when they helped their clients with major technical issues. They came to understand that in such circumstances, they are often more likely than sales personnel to find a thankful open door to new commercial suggestions.

The outcome? The technical engineers realized that heart, soul, and brand can be communicated along with measurements and know-how. Managers came away with a better understanding of the job parameters their engineers needed to foster that communication.

GET INTO THE CHARACTER

Imagine that your company is like a theater. You are going to put on a theater performance with your personnel. So, you have to arrive at clear-cut agreements. First, what production are you going to put on? Second, who will be playing a role? And then, what is the setup of decor, light, and sound going to be like? Finally you also need a promotional activity to make the performance known throughout the country.

The performance you're going to put on is your brand. Your brand should say something to customers: What is it? Is it a promise? Is it provocative? Reassuring? What is the story your brand is telling? Why does the story matter? Who will care if your story is told? Can your brand solve a problem? Can you describe the problem and the solution? Who are the people in your company that are helping the brand express itself? Why are they important to the brand's story? What role do they play?

For the sake of discussion, let's say your performance is *The Three Musketeers.* You will have to clearly agree on who, for example, the Three Musketeers in your organization are. You will have to arrange this well, as losing a musketeer during the dress rehearsal "because it's not his thing anymore" is not an option. Moreover, you are the director, so everything you have to arrange on the stage will have to happen ahead of time and not during the performance. You will also have to have mapped out all the other roles very clearly, and everybody who has a part in the performance will have to be in full agreement. In getting ready, everybody will have to be prepared to help out and rehearse.

With actors, you often see the passion that goes beyond their prescribed working hours. For them, it's all about perfecting the performance, the passion for presentation, the passion for acting. So, they don't shut the door behind themselves at five o'clock. A goal has been set—the actual start of a presentation—and that goal has to be attained. Finally the performance is to take place. The decor will have to make sense, light and sound will have to be finely attuned, everybody will have to know their part, and the audience will have to come flocking in thanks to well-adapted PR and a well-adapted marketing campaign.

Can you map out your brand as you would a play? What role do your front-line employees play? Do they have their script? Have they had adequate time to study it? Do they have the proper stage and props and lighting? Can they "get into character" and be comfortable their roles. Can they take what they know of their roles and make it a part of themselves; can they be authentic?

Some companies we've worked with have embraced this approach; their managers immediately grasp how to align the brand with their employees' roles, and how the "production" should flow when the audience arrives.

Other companies find that the approach uncovers a host of internal contradictions about the brand or areas in which large numbers of employees have never conceived of themselves as connecting with the brand in any way. For these companies, we encourage managers to begin to educate employees by thinking as simply as possible about the message they are trying to send. What lies at the core of the brand? Can it be summed up in text that can be read in one minute or less? At some companies, we take another step and move from that single minute of text to a mime presentation. Can the company convey the brand convincingly through nonverbal communication? Can the company deliver a message that touches on the essence of the brand on a purely cognitive level?

Customers quickly discover for themselves when "friendliness and client satisfaction" are not linked with authenticity. Ultimately, it is the customer who feels the fallout when managers and employees are constantly goaded to attain higher sales figures and are put through the wringer to perform even better each year. When a manager asks, "How are you doing?" to an employee, but really means "How are your sales doing?" you can expect that employee to say "How are you doing?" to a customer, but mean "Hurry up; I have to move on to the next person in line."

The new is impossible without the old; I'll grant you that. Management teams can't ask employees to interact in an authentic way with customers unless the fundamentals are in place in terms of product, market, strategy, and organizational infrastructure. But it is time for a soft revolution, when quality truly comes to mean much more than reducing error.

PART III

Case-Based Insights

The customer walked into the store, admiring the new design, the wider aisles, the cleaner smell. "This place has really changed," she thought. She went up to the customer service desk and was greeted with a smile. "How can I help you today?" the staff member asked her. "I'm looking for a particular toy," the customer explained. She described the toy and said she wasn't sure of the name.

The customer service representative said, "I think we had those; let me check for you." She led the customer to an aisle at the far end of the store and called to another employee who appeared to be stocking shelves. "Do we have any more of those toys?" she said, using the product's name.

"Nope," came the reply.

"Nope," the customer service representative said to the customer, smiling.

"Well, can you tell me when you might get some in?" the customer asked.

"Hey Diane, are we getting any in?" the rep asked the other employee.

"Nope," said the other employee. Then, as an afterthought, "We might have some in now, in the back, but I can't go check; I'm on the floor."

The customer service rep turned, still smiling, to relay the reply to the customer; but the customer was already walking away, waving, saying a half-hearted, "thanks anyway."

Some companies seem to be able to engage their front-line employees thoroughly. These employees are true ambassadors of the company's brand; their actions engage and persuade customers, even when they're not able to meet a specific customer need.

There is no single "secret recipe" for this kind of engagement. These next chapters offer insights from several different companies with proven success at the front lines, in the hope that one or more of their styles and techniques resonates for your business.

CHAPTER 10

Once upon a Time at San Juan Regional Medical Center

**Gary Adamson, B. Joseph Pine II,
Tom Van Steenhoven, and Jodi Kroupa**

Once upon a time. When strung together, these four words are among the most powerful in the English language. Their very mention starts a vivid movie in our minds full of colorful places, wild animals, vile villains, and courageous heroines all wrapped around an important life-changing lesson and served in bed with warm cookies and milk. And even though most of us have a hard time these days remembering what we had yesterday for breakfast, we can recall every detail about these stories some three, four, or even five decades later. We also remember the people from whence such stories came—Hans Christian Andersen, Lewis Carroll, Mother Goose. Just the names are enough to give a warm feeling inside. In fact, even though Jacob and Wilhelm Grimm were famous professors at the renowned Berlin Academy and spent more than 40 years of their lives compiling the German Dictionary, that's not what they're known for. They did one other thing, almost a hobby really. They collected and rewrote folk tales—stories that had been handed down over generations. They compiled them into a book called. . . . Oh, you know about *Grimm's Fairy Tales*? Out of all the many things the Brothers Grimm did, what you remember are their stories. Interesting.

What do stories and their uncanny ability to stay vividly in our memories have to do with corporate strategy, company transformation, and employee engagement? Everything! Let us explain. In our work we help senior management of companies, large and small, make the fundamental changes necessary to succeed in the experience economy.[1] And because experiences require a different set of management capabilities, as well as a different view of what the company actually produces, delivers, or sells, we are not dealing with incremental change. The business transformations we guide involve conceiving and "themeing" a whole new set of economic offerings, mass customizing these offerings for each of our client's customers, developing the partnerships and technology to extend these experiences beyond the usual points of customer contact, redesigning the physical space that the company inhabits to more effectively stage these experiences, re-conceiving the way employees are recruited (we use the term audition) to perform their new experience roles, and building a comprehensive corporate university that teaches in the new way to every employee and business partner the company has. Then the hard work starts!

No matter how well conceived and funded our plan, no matter how committed our leaders, no matter how pressing the market forces, this experience economy transformation is doomed if we can't vibrantly engage all the people in the company that will be needed to carry it out. And that's everyone. They need a new concept of the company and their place in it. They need a new context for how the company will compete effectively in this new economy. And most important, they need to know that this is not another "flavor-of-the-month" change program that leaves almost as quickly as it arrives. The employees need meaning, emotion, and belief. In short, they need a good story.

WHY NOT A MEMO?

Conventional wisdom says that when confronted with a major organizational change—one that shakes the very foundations of how the company does business—top executives need to leave their offices and venture out "among the people" to make sure that everyone understands. Memos are written, speechwriters summoned, PowerPoint slides prepared, and communications plans developed all to get everyone "on the same page," "rowing in the same direction," "eating the same dog food," or "singing off the same song sheet." (Hopefully not, however, "drinking the same Kool-Aid.") E-mails are sent, meetings called, retreats planned, annual reports prepared, and newsletter articles published, all to ensure that "at the end of the day our new value proposition and business model have been ingrained in the culture," or something like that. Then leaders pack up their stuff, go back to their offices, and wait to see their seeds of change take root and blossom. And they wait. And they wait. And they wait. Usually, not much happens and that leaves managers scratching their heads, ordering books like the one you are holding in your hands, and lamenting to each other about how much people hate to change. In other words, there's a whole lot more talking about change, identifying what needs to change, meeting about how to change things, and writing about the coming changes than there is actual changing going on. And each failed attempt just makes it more difficult to succeed the next time.

Why doesn't this approach work? And why, after so many failed attempts, do leaders still use it? Let's examine the underlying assumptions upon which the "Just Tell 'Em" approach is based. First, it assumes that the front-line employees have the needed context and background information required to understand major changes in strategic direction. (They don't. Often times even the managers, who have much more information, confess that they don't even understand what it all means.) Second, it assumes that employees totally accept the decisions of their top executives. (They don't. Especially after so many "major" change efforts have come and gone.) Third, "Just Tell 'Em" assumes that employees don't have valid ideas of their own about where the company should be going. (They do. And while they may be forced to accept the conclusions of management, they will still draw their own conclusions and act accordingly.) Fourth, this approach assumes that change is basically an information issue and that if they just knew the reasons why it would be good to change, they'd change. (They won't. Ask any smoker or overweight person about the accuracy of this assumption. Change is as much about relationships, emotions, and gut feel as it is about facts.) And, last, this approach assumes that no "fluff" or entertainment value is needed; because the subject matter is so important and the people presenting it so noteworthy, employees will pay attention even if it's boring. (They won't. This flies in the face of that old saying that "Great teaching is one-fourth preparation and three-fourths theater.") Zero for Five: that's a bad night in any sport, especially the sport of strategic change.

So if it doesn't work, why do so many leaders keep doing it? It may be as simple as: it's all we know. When you received your management training—both in school and on the job—we'll bet there wasn't any on the power of memorable, engaging experiences, or on the whys and hows of storytelling. It's hard for even the most courageous leader to bet the future of the company on something he or she doesn't know how to do. Let's see if we can't fix that.

A GOOD STORY

There are many genres of stories and many different styles used by their tellers, but a good story always combines conflict, drama, suspense, plot twists, symbols, characters, triumph over odds, and sometimes even humor—all to do two things: capture your imagination and make you feel.

A great story draws you in, places you at its center, connects to the emotional core of your being, and doesn't let go until its meaning has become a permanent part of you. (Why else do you think it was possible to accurately transmit all of human history, before there were printing presses, through oral stories?) And therein lies why stories must become an integral part of corporate strategy: they are the experience that lets strategy be understood at a visceral level. To be effective, strategy must not just inform, it must inspire. And people are *never* inspired by reason alone. "The heart always holds hands with the head." That's why the "Just Tell 'Em" approach fails. It totally overlooks the role emotion and meaning play in any life-altering action. And if strategy isn't about altering the life of your company, why do it?

Stories are better for sharing knowledge and ideas than PowerPoint presentations and dry memos. They develop relationships by helping everyone realize we all have issues in common. Stories can crystallize common values and beliefs. They can build stronger teams and a stronger sense of community. Stories invite people to bring the "whole person" to work (heart and head), and therefore elicit much more thorough perspectives and meaningful commitments. They can create a platform for more aspirational work and can make each employee feel more valued. In short, stories have the potential to revitalize the way we do business.

By this point you may be thinking, "This all sounds great but is there any proof that it works?" Indeed there is. As Stephen Denning, former program director at The World Bank said in the introduction to his book, *The Springboard: How Storytelling Ignites Action in Knowledge-Era Organizations*, "Time after time, when faced with the task of persuading a group of managers or front-line staff in a large organization to get enthusiastic about a major change, I found that storytelling was the only thing that worked."[2] Now let us tell you a story. It may have happened once upon a time, but it also happens to be true.

FOCUSING ON EMPLOYEES

"It was a real trying period," says Steve Altmiller President and CEO of San Juan Regional Medical Center, reflecting back on his early years at the 175-bed, sole-community provider in Farmington, New Mexico. "There I was, a new CEO at a historically strong community hospital and suddenly everything was out of sync. We were taking lots of financial hits; our earnings were down, our hospital-sponsored health plan was going bankrupt, unions were trying to organize our nurses, and we were making many operational and management changes that introduced lots of anxiety. It seemed like everything we talked about was negative, one problem after another. My board said we had to find a way to focus on something positive."

Steve decided to engage a top group of his leaders, directors, board members, and physicians in developing a comprehensive experience strategy that would change everything. Shortly into its two-year project, it began calling itself the Galileo Group, for its goal was to discover a new and more personally meaningful center of the healthcare universe. In the midst of their work the members made a radical decision: they would focus first not on the patient experience but rather on the *employee* experience. "We can't consistently provide the most personal patient experience until we can consistently provide the most personal, healing professional experience. If you expect to be successful in individualizing the patient experience you'd better get good at individualizing to the employee," Altmiller told us. "Our entire patient experience redesign will start with an exclusive focus on the employee experience. We're going to try to personalize everything from recruitment to retirement because we think it will do more than anything else to help our employees understand what we want for patients. And in these times of staff shortages and heavy competition for the best people, it would be a good strategy even if we weren't planning to do it for patients. As it is, we've come to believe that individualizing the experience will ensure our future success. You've got to be able to do it not just when times are good but when times are hard. We're not just following a trend—we're putting it in everything we do."

So a new mission, vision, and philosophy were developed, a new personalized benefit program put in place, and a completely new healing environment designed into the facility expansion project. Many other initiatives were being readied while the rollout of the first phase of changes was begun. And then something quite unexpected happened. All the hard work, all the careful planning, all the innovative design—all of it resulted in *confusion,* not cohesion. "I realized pretty quickly," Altmiller relates, "that while we had done a good job of defining 'the what,' we were doing a bad job of communicating 'the why.' If we were ever going to connect the dots, it wasn't going to be with another PowerPoint presentation. Instead we needed a 'what's the point' experience."

RAIDERS OF THE LOST ART

And so began the work on something that would change everything—the work on a story. It became known as "The Raiders of the Lost Art." As the name implies, through this adventure story we were looking for something that had been lost, namely the art of personalized healthcare. The story took place in three distinct lands: the land of Medicus (medical professionals), the land of Communia (regional community), and the land of Patiem (patients). In each land, operational statistics, industry trends, competitive issues, and organizational initiatives relating specifically to the subject of that area were presented.

To get a quick sampling of the lessons presented in each land, let's take a quick journey. In the land of Medicus, employees learned how the baby-boom generation affects not only the patient population they treat, but also the peers with whom they work on a daily basis. In the land of Communia, employees took an in-depth look at the hospital's community satisfaction results and discussed how they could change processes and/or work styles to improve these results in the future. In the land of Patiem, employees learned of the exciting new plans built into the facility expansion project, which would provide a unique healing environment for employees as well as all patients and their families.

These encounters were enlivened by an environment filled with props, via an Indiana Jones-like facilitator (and assistance from manager guides) and through map icons (landslides, volcanoes, rope bridges, mirages, a treasure chest, hidden caves, a bottomless pit, deserts, oceans, secret passageways, and lush gardens—to name just a few).

But the Raiders of the Lost Art story was not only told; more important it was *asked*. At each map icon, when some new challenge or initiative was presented, a series of small group discussions were held that involved every employee in the session in a deeper examination.

Questions like, "Does this surprise you?", "How do you think this will affect us?", "Are we doing enough?", and "What else would you do?" engaged employees in strategy work as never before. And as the word of the exciting work spread throughout the hospital, more and more employees wanted to be involved. In the end, nearly 70 percent of San Juan Regional's 1,300 employees attended the voluntary daylong sessions. Almost 900 distinct process, program, and facility suggestions were captured and then analyzed, with approximately half of them acted on.

And all of a sudden, the connection between management and employee changed. Skepticism, fear, and apathy departed. Understanding, excitement, and a sense of partnership ensued. How do we know? There are both soft and hard measures. Morale improved, turnover plummeted, and employee satisfaction scores climbed dramatically. New initiatives were understood and embraced; for example, more than 80 percent of the employees have signed up for the customized benefits program that is more personally relevant *and* less expensive to the provider. Further, San Juan Regional opened a Child Discovery Center, with almost 70 percent of its capacity filled by employees' kids.

There was one other thing. (And while it wasn't the primary focus of the story, it was a significant factor in the future of the medical center.) You might remember that San Juan Regional had developed plans for a major facility expansion and renovation to help fulfill its new mission, vision, and philosophy and to create a state-of-the-art healing environment. Many of the suggestions that came out of the Raider's story, in fact, were focused on this new facility. Unfortunately, the hospital could raise only about half the money required to complete the project. San Juan Regional could go to its community for financial support through bond issues or tax initiatives. But the last three times it had

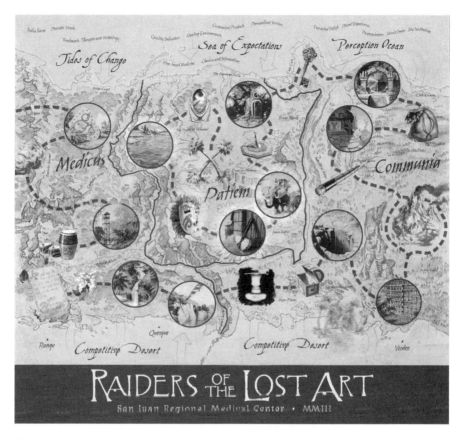

This reproduction of the Raiders of the Lost Art story map highlights the adventure San Juan Regional Medical Center's employees embarked on during the day-long session. The journey began in the upper left corner, in the land of Medicus, continued through Communia, and finally ended at the crossed palm trees in the land of Patiem. Each icon on the dotted trail included various learning and discussion points about which the employees shared their input and suggestions for making change.

done so—all for much less money than was needed this time—it had been turned down.

The Raiders of the Lost Art story sessions were completed about four months before the gross receipts tax election. Then something amazing happened. Largely without any help from management, employees began to talk to each other, to their families, and to their friends. And their tone was enthusiastic; they talked about what the project was and, more important, what it meant. They talked about why it was important to patients, families, healthcare professionals, local businesses, even the entire community. In other words, they talked about everything they had learned in—and contributed to—the story.

When Election Day finally arrived, the air was filled with great anticipation, but also great anxiety. What would happen if the voters said no again? How would the hospital ever fulfill its aspirations? And with new hospitals being built in surrounding communities, could it ever compete successfully should a no vote occur?

As the votes were counted, it was obvious something major had changed. When the counting was done, San Juan Regional's tax initiative had received 84 percent of the vote! That's right, more than four of five voters supported a tax initiative for more money than the combined total of the initiatives they had voted down every time in the past.

Construction has now begun on a new facility—a new stage really—that will let San Juan Regional provide a much more compelling healthcare experience. An experience that lives up to its new mission, vision, and philosophy. One that will let it recapture the Lost Art of Personalized Healthcare. In other words, a very happy ending indeed. Except for one thing—it's not the end. Now, as Paul Harvey would say, let us tell you "the rest of the story."

RIDDLE OF THE SPHINX

With so much success, it would be easy to rest on one's laurels. After all, since all employees now understand—but wait a minute, they don't understand, at least not totally. For since the day of the last Raiders' session things have changed dramatically and will continue to do so. Therefore there is a need for another story, and down the road another one after that, and one after that. Steve Altmiller looks at it this way, "When we decided to do the Raiders story, I looked at it as R&D. At worst, we would learn something, and what we had done up to that point wasn't working anyway. At best, we would build a whole new capacity that would enable us to do new things better, faster, and, ultimately, less expensively. So it seemed it was worth the risk. When Raiders was such a big success, I wanted to use that success as a building block. I didn't want anyone to see it as a one-time thing done primarily to pass the gross receipts tax. That would have missed the whole point of what we learned. We learned a whole new way for management and employees to work together to make dramatic new things happen. So we have committed to this type of storytelling and feedback to be done every 18 months. It's just the way we're going to do things from now on."

And so a second story was prepared and told, this one entitled "The Riddle of the Sphinx." Through solving various riddles and an anagram posed by an ancient Egyptian Sphinx, San Juan Regional employees solved the many confusions that plague an industry as complicated as

The second employee storytelling journey included another table-sized map, entitled the Riddle of the Sphinx. The pyramid entrance in the lower left corner led employees along a winding, sometimes treacherous excursion through the serpentine hallways. Various hieroglyphics and riddles were solved along the way, to open secret passageways and reveal hidden staircases—creating yet another engaging and memorable experiential learning lab.

healthcare. Communications confusions, staffing confusions, process confusions, patient-expectation confusions, and technology confusions were all addressed through the story.

For example, the employees' first riddle revolved around various communications confusions such as an in-depth look at the most recent employee satisfaction survey (wherein communications between employees and their managers ranked 4 percent below the national norm). The next riddle comprised all of the confusions related to staffing. Here, employees learned about the newest work/life balance programs recently put into place by the hospital. Riddle three considered an assortment of

"X" marks the spot. This is the main entrance to The Riddle
of the Sphinx journey. Attendees enter beneath the crossed
palms into an Egyptian pyramid.

process confusions. During this stage, employees brainstormed ideas to
more effectively treat patients despite ever-increasing industry regula-
tions. The next riddle addressed numerous patient-expectation confusions. In one example, employees were asked for ideas in creating
strategies to decrease the number of patients who seek treatment elsewhere because they were unaware that San Juan Regional offered those
specific treatments. The final riddle asked employees to uncover technology confusions by conceiving new ways to more effectively train
staff members on increasingly complicated technologies throughout the
system. Best of all, as these riddles and confusions were addressed and

Once inside the pyramid, attendees immediately become immersed in the experience, as they recognize authentic hieroglyphics surrounding them on every wall.

discussed, employee ideas were meticulously recorded so they can be used in future initiatives.

From an environment and employee engagement point of view, Riddle of the Sphinx was an even bigger production than Raiders. "We wanted to capture the same element of surprise and amazement we had in Raiders, and we knew that would require an even more elaborate experience, since Raiders had raised everybody's expectations so high," said Altmiller.

And so it was. The Sphinx story took over a recently closed elementary school and transformed it into ancient Egypt. The Raiders story ended under crossed palm trees ("X" marked the spot), so that's where the

Through the use of dimensional props such as the period-specific tent, canteen, and knapsack shown here, attendees can suspend reality and become part of the story. The journey is coming alive!

A preshow video sets of tone of the journey, playing simultaneously on five screens located around the room. To further pique attendees' interest, the video features some of the same props that surround them, along with "actors" who are actually San Juan Regional employees. A customized music track keeps the adrenaline pumping, while final scenes show a Sphinxlike creature who poses the opening riddle, along with a challenge to solve that riddle or accept defeat!

Participants are guided through the learning process by a trained table guide and a video flipchart. Fabric walls, again covered in hieroglyphics, separate the learning tables not only to provide privacy but also to develop team camaraderie. The groups were separated by Crews: Tet, Menkaure, Ramses, Khafre, Khufu, Cheops, and Anubis, each named after famous Egyptian pharaohs. As a memento of the journey, each participant was given a "Crew" bandana.

What would a pyramid be without its own sarcophagus? To further immerse participants in the experience, they were encouraged to explore the artistic details of this 8-foot long, life-sized prop. See the final picture and caption for a true understanding of the sarcophagus' importance and ultimate discovery of the story.

Throughout the day's learnings, attendees are posed six different riddles, the answers to which (the letter "e," few, stars, wind, fire, and time) are later unscrambled and used to solve a floor-to-ceiling anagram.

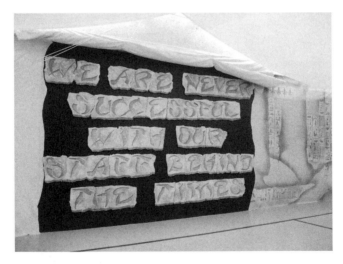

The solved anagram provides attendees with yet another cryptic message. To understanding its meaning, everyone must watch the closing video and discover the answer to the ultimate riddle: "who is the pharaoh entombed within the pyramid . . . who is the possessor of light?" The final answer is, of course, each one of them. They are the ones who can bring light and energy to their work everyday. They are the answer to it all—every employee at San Juan Regional Medical Center!

Sphinx story started. A Disney-esque preshow and postshow video was produced to engage employees in the storyline before the work began and to summarize the story's key moral once it was over.

To get an idea of the power of the immersive environment in capturing the employee's imagination and making them feel—the key requirements of any story—just look at the photos in this chapter. It's a long way from the PowerPoint presentation in the conference room off the cafeteria, isn't it? Much of the reaction to the Riddle of the Sphinx echoed what Diana Candelaria, VP Professional and Personal Development, told us: "People are saying they're amazed; that it's even better than Raiders—and they didn't think that was possible."

Steve Altmiller summarizes his experience with storytelling this way, "Before we started our storytelling work, the reaction to most of the things in our experience strategy plan was 'You can't do that in Farmington.' After Raiders and Sphinx, we are doing all of the things in the plan. That's a big difference."

So what's the moral of this story on stories?

Don't just spend countless hours, valuable brain cells, and barrels full of money doing the research, analysis, goal-setting, and implementation planning necessary to come up with an industry-altering strategy. If you want the strategy to actually take hold—if you want it to change your world—then weave it into a compelling and memorable story. It's something all that hard work needs and deserves. Because when more leaders immerse their employees in compelling and inspirational strategy stories, more companies will live happily ever after.

NOTES

1. B. Joseph Pine II and James H. Gilmore, *The Experience Economy: Work Is Theatre & Every Business a Stage* (Boston: Harvard Business School Press, 1999).

2. Stephen Denning, *The Springboard: How Storytelling Ignites Action in Knowledge-Era Organizations* (Woburn, Mass.: Butterworth-Heinemann, 2000), xiii.

CHAPTER 11

Strategy and Style: Len Roberts at RadioShack

V. Kasturi Rangan and Marie Bell

At any retail enterprise, the store and the merchandise are rarely the sole manifestation of the company's strategy. These elements have to be animated by the front-line store personnel to make the company's overall strategy come alive. Often, though, something is lost in translation, and the strategy—set at the uppermost levels of the organization—never achieves its potential and comes alive for employees or customers.

Not so at RadioShack, one of the leading consumer electronics retailers in the United States, with 2004 sales of about $4.81 billion. At this company, the big-picture strategy has been atomized into "store-sized pellets" for consistent execution across the chain of nearly 7,000 stores all over the United States. Put another way, RadioShack has successfully made 7,000 carbon copies of a top-level strategy for execution across a vast chain, although several layers of management, each with their own interpretations and biases in implementing the top management's vision, lie between the top level and the shop floor.

One reason RadioShack has been able to do this is that the company has deliberately made its strategic message simple and straightforward, so there is little scope for distortion. But RadioShack has also made a particular effort to deliver that message with authority and credibility from the top. In fact, at RadioShack, during the last decade, 1994 to 2004, the CEO, Leonard Roberts (Len Roberts) himself, played an important role in disseminating the company's strategy across the organization. He saw himself as an ambassador of the company's strategy, both internally and externally. And as such, he personally conveyed his vision to two key groups of stakeholders within the firm: the store managers and the immediate layer of management reporting directly to him.[1]

Roberts believed that if the strategy was received and embraced by these two groups, assuming it was a good one, it would then be successfully implemented. The store managers would execute with customers and Roberts's team would develop the plans and policies that would support the field with the products and tools they needed to be successful. He took a classical approach to combining communication pull with policy push, but in doing so, managed to mold a distinctive style, where strategy pronouncements were designed and delivered from the top, and then backed up and reinforced through field level execution programs. Many times the strategizing itself involved development of field level training programs and tools, but Roberts made it a point to leave a lot of individual room for second and third layers of management to flesh out the details.

Such a style of strategy dissemination is most useful when the front-line workers are an extension of the company's strategy—in retail establishments, financial service institutions, airlines, educational institutions, and others. Moreover, the style adopted by Len Roberts enables an accelerated implementation, because intermediate layers of management have to react almost as fast as the front-line workers demand an execution plan. Therefore the implementation is often aided by front-line input. If an organization knows how to cope and build on that input, it improves its chances for success. Although strategy itself does not change as frequently, in many kinds of businesses the positioning with respect to competitors' product offerings does change rapidly. Take for example the role of merchandise at retail. If one promises the latest in fashion, or lowest in prices, or the highest standards in quality, these are dependent on what the competition is doing. A nimble business might find it expedient to lay out the nuances of the new positioning and get its quick acceptance through the mechanism of "pull combined with push" execution. The advantage is that the front-line employees, who carry out the strategy, buy into the new positioning. The resulting boost in morale often provides the energy for the strategy adaptation.

It would trivialize the complexities of strategy formulation and execution if one were to attempt to link this unique dissemination style to the success or failure of strategy at RadioShack. The purpose of this article, therefore, is not to pretend to make that causal link, but rather to describe an execution style that has many appealing features given the contingency of the business model. We offer in Table 11.1 the aggregate financial performance data. In general, we believe this data bolsters the credibility of the effectiveness of such a style in implementing strategy, but that is not the main thrust of the piece. Our goal is to demonstrate the three phases of RadioShack's strategy and how its CEO Len Roberts carefully orchestrated its connection to field level personnel for quick implementation free of distortion

Table 11.1
RadioShack 1984–2004

Year-ended Dec. 1984 (Tandy)		Year-ended Dec. 1994		Year-ended Dec. 2004	
Sales: $2,784 billion		Sales: $2.853 billion		Sales: $4.469 billion	
US Stores:		US Stores:		US Stores:	
Company owned:	4,717	Company owned:	4,598	Company owned:	5,046
Dealer owned:	2,064	Dealer owned:	2,005	Dealer owned:	1,788
Total:	6,781	Total:	6,603	Total:	6,834
Average Store size: n/a		Average store size: 2,350 sq. ft.		Average store size: 2,529 sq. ft.	
Sales Mix:		Sales Mix:		Sales Mix:	
Consumer electronics: 54.3%		Consumer electronics: 45.4%		Wireless 33.8%	
Electronic parts, accessories & specialty equipment 12.1%		Electronic parts, accessories & specialty equipment 36.0%		Accessories 20.8%	
				Modern home 14.5%	
				Personal electronics 13.5%	
PCs, peripherals, software & accessories 33.6%		PCs, peripherals, software & accessories 12.0%		Power (batteries, chargers) 6.4%	
				Service & Technical 8.6%	
				Retail support operations service plans & other 2.4%	
		Other 6.6%			
Total 100.0%		Total 100.0%		Total 100.0%	

Source: Tandy and RadioShack.

AMERICA'S TECHNOLOGY STORE GETS UNPLUGGED

The RadioShack story began in Dorchester (a subdivision of Boston, Massachusetts) in 1921 when the first store opened to meet the needs of the emerging electronics of the day—ham radios. In those early days, RadioShack was the place for the newest technology with AM and FM tuners and innovative transistor radios. During subsequent decades RadioShack expanded across the United States, continuing to offer emerging radio technology as well as new consumer electronics. Throughout the 1970s, RadioShack rode the wave of technology with the EC-100 Pocket Calculator, Tandy's TRS personal computer and the first affordable cordless telephone. In addition to core technology products, RadioShack gained renown as the store that had every conceivable gadget required to hook up and run electronics. No matter what the situation, RadioShack would have the item needed.

By the 1980s, however, RadioShack's glory days seemed behind them. The pace of technological innovation in consumer electronics diminished. Several years passed without a technology breakthrough. Products such as computers became increasingly commoditized, resulting in reduced prices and eroding margins. Additionally, and more profoundly, the 1980s saw the rise of "big box" retailers. Consumer electronics retailers such as Circuit City, Best Buy, and CompUSA successfully launched and developed 20,000 to 24,000 sq ft stores—10 times the size of an average RadioShack store. As these stores became the model for electronics retailing, RadioShack was increasingly seen as a relic of the past. Indeed, RadioShack's parent, Tandy Corporation, a historical driver of RadioShack's innovation, diversified into nonelectronics businesses such as the Bombay furniture store chain and ready-to-assemble furniture by O'Sullivan. Moreover, when it finally refocused on the consumer electronics business, Radio Shack's parent too seemed to veer toward the big box culture. Tandy developed its big Computer City store format (25,000 sq ft stores) and even bigger Incredible Universe stores (186,000 sq ft stores with 85,000 stock keeping units, or SKUs), leaving the dependable RadioShack as a cash cow to fuel these concepts.

In the early 1990s, Tandy tried to recapture RadioShack's innovative past by positioning RadioShack as "America's Technology Store." By that time, however, given the advances in technology this was not a position that RadioShack could pull off.[2] It was not in any position to offer the glittering array of TVs in a "wall-sized" merchandize display. There was no physical room for such an offering, or for that matter enough space to accommodate a depth of inventory to cater to consumers' wide-ranging tastes. For many, RadioShack had become an anachronism of an earlier era of retailing and technology. The meaning of technology leadership had evolved from one of providing components for consumer customization, to one of product design and mass marketing. Customers could go to any number of "big box retailers" and get a broad selection of brand name electronics at competitive prices. There was no need, nor for that matter any incentive to go to RadioShack, unless a product failed and the customers wanted to buy a replacement cord or connect it to another piece.

RECONNECTING RADIOSHACK

You've got Questions. We've got Answers.
Our mission is to demystify technology in every neighborhood in America.

When the 44-year-old Roberts became president of RadioShack in 1993, he was an outsider, coming from the restaurant industry where he had revitalized Arby's and Shoney's restaurant chains.[3] "RadioShack was an icon that was dying quickly from profit and sales erosion. When you have a small store with limited selection and all you are doing is promoting your product as cheaper than your competition, you are going to lose relevance. That's what was happening—RadioShack was losing relevancy," noted Roberts soon after his arrival.[4] Yet Roberts viewed RadioShack as having three major assets that could be leveraged: its market coverage, its product assortment, and its employees.

For all its loss of relevance, RadioShack had an undeniably unique market coverage position. With its almost 7,000 locations (about 5,000 company-owned and 2,000 franchised stores), RadioShack's store count exceeded that of Wal-Mart, K-Mart, and Sears combined. RadioShack had ubiquitous market coverage: 95 percent of Americans lived or worked within five minutes of a RadioShack store or dealer, one out of every three households in the United States purchased RadioShack products each year. On average, a million customers visited RadioShack every day.

Unlike many franchise organizations that rigidly apply store standards, Radio Shack was more flexible, allowing for the difference between metropolitan and rural markets. RadioShack's company-owned stores tended to be in the larger metropolitan markets, with rural locations served by the dealer system. Dealers paid RadioShack a minimal, one-time set-up fee (about $70,000) to operate the store, and purchased inventory annually from RadioShack. Dealer stores were not required to be freestanding locations and were frequently located in hardware stores, grocery stores, and auto parts stores in rural and smaller markets. Indeed, RadioShack had designed a 500-sq ft store with its top 1,800 products, called RadioShack Select, specifically designed for dealers to operate within the confines of a larger retail establishment. As a result, even in rural markets, there was always a convenient RadioShack, with the big box retailers generally providing a less-convenient option.

RadioShack's inventory was also unique. The standard RadioShack store was approximately 2,400 sq ft and carried more than 3,800 items in its inventory. The merchandise assortment was customized for each location, with a mix of core and select items. Core merchandise of about 1,000 SKUs was found in every RadioShack store. Select merchandise was based on an individual store's open-to-buy merchandise history (the difference between planned annual purchases and stock already ordered). Because of its assortment, RadioShack had unusually low inventory turns. A big box retailer might turn its inventory six times per year, but typically RadioShack inventory turns were about two times per year. Len Roberts explained, "Ours is a slow-turn business because of our parts and accessory business. We may have a particular part in a store that doesn't move for two years. But having that part is the reason why people come to us in the first place."[5]

RadioShack's third asset was its employees. Typical RadioShack stores were small and staffed by a store manager and usually two to three full-time equivalent employees. Commission was a significant part of employee compensation. Staff at the store had unique sales skills. Rather than selling the "box" that was sold at a big box retailer, the RadioShack employee sold the parts that connected the box to other boxes or fixed the "box" when it became inoperable. RadioShack's people then were electronics problem solvers rather than product sellers. As Roberts once noted:

Our training program is so substantive ...training is very important to us. But it really has a lot to do with the kinds of people we hire. We just hire people—it's not so much what they know about technology. We hire people that just love customer service. They love helping people out with their problems. We teach them a lot about the technology. And those are our best people.[6]

Ultimately, Roberts's revitalization strategy was simple yet profound: enhance the current business by changing it from a product/technology orientation to a service business and provide a product assortment that met the needs of technology customers, especially technology customers mystified by the very technology that they desired.

"YOU'VE GOT QUESTIONS, WE'VE GOT ANSWERS"

The cornerstone of Roberts's strategy for RadioShack was a change in the perception of the RadioShack store. Unlike the early days of RadioShack, customers generally didn't go to RadioShack for the most cutting edge technology; other stores had emerged to serve that niche. Rather RadioShack, was the place customers went when they needed answers about technology. Roberts understood that the technology in its stores was not the draw for customers, but rather employees' ability to solve technology questions created store traffic and ultimately store sales. The new customer service mantra was reinforced with the demise of RadioShack's longtime slogan of "America's Technology Store" in favor of "You've Got Questions, We've Got Answers." Roberts described RadioShack's mission as "demystifying technology for the mass market," reflecting a belief that customers were confused by technology and were desperately seeking a nonintimidating place to buy electronics products and services that served both technophiles and technophobes. The mantra of "You've Got Questions, We've Got Answers," became the campaign slogan at RadioShack all the way down from Len Roberts to the store display. It was the headline in all of RadioShack's advertising campaigns, and the beauty of it was that it represented a statement of the retail chain's business strategy!

Service became the centerpiece of RadioShack's retail offering, with Roberts setting the tone by telling his direct reports that RadioShack people "either serve customers or serve someone who does." Roberts lifted up the profile of RadioShack's people, encouraging them to look "beyond the parts-and-pieces clutter and envision themselves as a neighborhood access point for technology-based services." Roberts commented:

When I looked at the RadioShack opportunity I saw a gold mine that just wasn't being exploited. The big box retailers were killing us. In my mind, that didn't make sense. RadioShack's salespeople were considered the most trusted and knowledge-able in the industry, and we had distribution points in every neighborhood in America. The problem was that RadioShack was merchandise driven rather than customer driven. We needed to look for areas with mass appeal, but also with mass confusion to eliminate the confusion and make the sale.[7]

Len Roberts and his team recognized and elevated the core qualities within its stores and employees that made a difference: trust, and exper-tise. Customers came to RadioShack looking for expertise and trusting that employees would be able to help them with their problems. Rather than minimizing this as a small part of the retail experience, Roberts celebrated it and got employees enthusiastic about their role. The "You've Got Questions, We've Got Answers" slogan created a sense of pride and accomplishment for employees and a sense of security for customers. Customers knew the RadioShack history and capabilities and, coupled with the effects of national advertising, became conditioned to going to RadioShack for the answers.

The parts and accessories business was the traditional business with which consumers most readily identified RadioShack. RadioShack was the dominant destination for small ticket (under $10) technology accessories such as connectors, fuses, surge protectors, batteries, antennae, phone jacks and cords, adapters, and handheld electronics. In addition to providing a seemingly unlimited supply of these ordinary parts, RadioShack also sup-plied the "hard" parts for the electronics devotee including diodes, capaci-tors, chips, transistors, and LCDs, plus the solder, wire, circuit boards, and tools to put them together. Generating 30 percent of sales with a 75 percent gross margin, the parts and accessories business was responsible for gen-erating about 80 percent of store traffic. As seen in the following quote, Roberts never overlooked or allowed his people to overlook the importance of the parts and accessory business:

The parts and accessories business, or "mother," as we like to call it, has been the essence of our business for our 75-year history. But we cannot take it for granted.

This business is not a self-service business. Customers do not come into our stores to search out the right part or connector; they expect that RadioShack's specialists will know what part is needed and be able to get it for them. That's our distinction. We provide exceptional service for a $3 item. Try getting that at a big box retailer.[8]

Roberts led the way with his strategy and employees followed—employees who would then sell to customers. The parts and accessories business was rejuvenated as sales associates were trained to give "complete answers and do the prework to accessorize the sale, so that it was not just one part but everything that the customer needed." RadioShack emphasized that the parts and accessories business was not a self-service business but, in service of the customer, where RadioShack built its distinctive customer perception.

UPSELL AND UPGRADE

Roberts emphasized that the parts and accessories business created a unique selling experience for RadioShack compared to its competitors. A RadioShack customer usually came to the store to buy a relatively inexpensive part or accessory. Based on that need, the customer interacted with the RadioShack specialist who then had an opportunity to enhance the sale by showing the customer an ancillary product and potentially even selling the customer a major piece of electronics. For example, a customer could come in looking for batteries for a portable CD player. In selling the batteries, the RadioShack salesperson could also sell additional parts and accessories such as a CD cleaner, a new pair of headphones, and even a new portable CD player with additional features. Such a sales process was the inverse of what happened in a large electronics store, where the focus was first on selling the high-ticket item, with little incentive thereafter to help the customer find the appropriate ancillary items.

But it wasn't just accessorizing the sale; Roberts was always selling and looking for new ways to sell RadioShack's core business. For example, in 1998, RadioShack rolled out the Power Zone to all RadioShack stores, reorganizing its scattered assortment of batteries (one of RadioShack's highest margin products) and related accessories into a central location. The Power Zone (that included almost every size battery, charger, surge protector, power strips, etc.) was featured along an 8- to 12-foot wall with its own revolving display kiosk. A Power Zone frequent shopper card was also reintroduced, offering customers up to 30 percent off batteries every day (starting at a 10 percent discount and increasing with the number of packages purchased) with an additional frequent-shopper bonus for up to $20 in free batteries.

Reflecting on the period, RadioShack characterized it as one where it rediscovered itself and learned to value the core services that the company offered to the people. Many proudly referred to the company as a Connector of Things (see Figure 11.1).

Roberts not only created his mantra but backed it up in communications and actions. Every year from 1995 to 1998, Roberts personally delivered a keynote address at the Peak of Performance meeting. Attendees were Roberts and his direct reports, the field store administrative organization, and managers from the high-performing stores that had earned their way to the meeting (by being in the top 20 percent of stores in terms of sales performance). Roberts reviewed past performance and communicated

Figure 11.1
(A) Parts and Accessories Anchor: Connecting "Things"

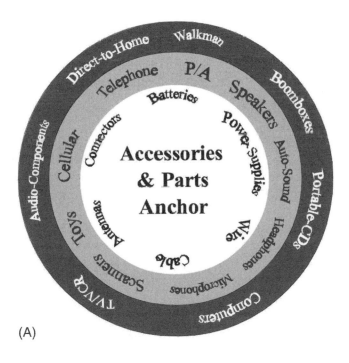

(A)

the next phase in his revitalization of the company. At that meeting he created the excitement and the buzz for the company for the forthcoming year. Robert's excitement was palpable and with it he created more and more pride among employees. They were no longer the lowly plugs and cable store; they were the "Connector of Things" that brought people and products together. These meetings proved an important communication vehicle. Videotapes of the meeting were sent to every store, and often when Roberts visited stores, the mangers and sales associates would ask him follow-up questions from that meeting. So it was clear to Len Roberts that his front-line employees were watching carefully for direction and guidance from Roberts himself. In fact, Roberts did not confine his communication to the Peak of Performance meeting, but worked tirelessly to be a presence in the stores with in-store visits and broadcast and satellite communications.

In his first two years as he worked on changing the focus of RadioShack from products to customer service, Roberts emphasized what he called the "three Ps" for RadioShack's continued growth: performance, perception, and people. Compensation and promotions systems were redesigned to incorporate the retention of the skilled people who provided the answers. Sales districts were realigned to reduce the span of control and bring managers closer to the stores and field personnel. The results were immediate. Between 1993 and 1995, sales grew $333 million, with a 31 percent increase in profitability. Roberts had successfully created "connections" between customers and RadioShack people and between RadioShack and profitability. From an operations perspective, store replenishment systems were reengineered, compensation plans redesigned, and merchandising plans reconfigured. The stores were also "cleaned up" to improve the visual impression that the customer received when entering the store.

THE NEXT PHASE—POA—CREATING ANCHORS AND OPPORTUNITIES

In 1996, the parts and accessories business, RadioShack's anchor to the customer, grew substantially, while communications began to emerge as a growth segment. Indeed, the growth in telecommunications led Roberts to announce the next phase of RadioShack's strategic plan called POA, a deliberate play on the acronym for plan of action, where RadioShack would continue to participate in certain segments, pursue opportunistic efforts, and focus on building new anchors, or growth engines such as telecommunications to complement the parts and accessories business.

The high-growth, technology-driven telecommunications segment proved to be an ideal *anchor* for RadioShack. Although customers were intrigued by the convenience of wireless telephones, they were confused and were looking for trusted advice regarding what telephone to buy and what service plan to enroll in—a ready opportunity for RadioShack to "provide answers" and demystify the myriad of product and service offerings. Although the technology made the transition to telecommunications, Roberts and RadioShack consistently adhered to their core message of providing answers.

The breakthrough step in building RadioShack's telecommunications anchor was a strategic alliance with Sprint, the third largest telecommunications company in the United States. Dave Edmondson, RadioShack's then COO, remarked, "At first we were pretty lukewarm about Sprint. They had no wireless, the brand had a so-so image, and they were a distant number three in the telecommunications market." He continued, "In these strategic alliances obviously the economics have to work, but it's also important that there is chemistry between the teams that they like and trust each other. With Sprint we not only had that rapport, but it was clear that we would be of strategic importance to them."[9] Under its 10-year agreement with Sprint, RadioShack received the exclusive right to sell Sprint's residential telephony products, and a nonexclusive right to sell its wireless digital PCS service. Additionally, to create awareness, Sprint participated in a multi-million dollar cooperative advertising campaign with RadioShack and invested in building an in-store display (a store within a store) devoted to its telephone offerings. RadioShack not only received the margins on the sale of the telephone, it also gained an income stream called a residual over the life of the customer. The residual was a predetermined percentage of the customer invoice that was received by the carrier, with mutually agreed adjustments over the life of the contract.

By 1998, RadioShack had been transformed to America's Telephone Store. As seen in Figure 11.2, with this transformation RadioShack had effectively extended the "connection theme" from solely a "connector of things, to a connector of things and a connector of people." As seen in Table 11.2, the connector of people strategy was enormously attractive to RadioShack, which reported incomes from residuals of about $34 million in 1998. This number had been virtually nonexistent in 1996. This performance is all the more noteworthy for the fixed cost of acquiring the customer happened only once, and from thereon the incremental costs were almost none, and the income falls right to the bottom line, and as Len Roberts noted, "Half of the people that buy wireless phone from us never intended to buy, but we eliminated the confusion and answered questions and made the sale."[10] RadioShack has continued to reap the success of the residual strategy through to the present, with Len Roberts remarking, "that the residual income stream represents a significant portion of our net income even today (2004)."

The focus remained on answers, but Roberts did not stop adding new products and new partners with Sprint. Alliances were created with

Figure 11.2
(A) Parts and Accessories Anchor: Connecting "Things"; (B) Telecommunications Anchor: Connecting "People"

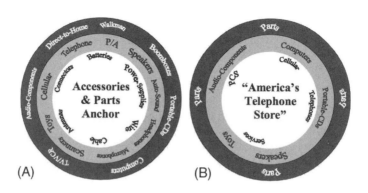

(A)   (B)

other branded consumer electronics companies. In personal computers, RadioShack created an alliance with Compaq that was built along the same model as the earlier Sprint agreement. Although there was increasing pressure on personal computer margins, RadioShack believed that it was important that the company continue to participate in this segment but within a distinct niche. Roberts and his team opted for an educational perspective of helping children—and with them their parents—demystify the computer. RadioShack believed that its education perspective fit well with its small store settings where customers would not be overwhelmed and would have the opportunity to ask questions about the systems.

In May 1999, RadioShack announced a strategic alliance with RCA. This alliance was expected not only to capture existing technologies but

Table 11.2
Residual Revenue by Product Category ($millions)

	1996	1997	1998	1999
Wireless	0	$4.7	$22.7	n/a
Long distance	0	0.4	2.3	n/a
DTH satellite	$1.2	4.2	8.0	n/a
Pagers/Other	0.1	0.2	1.0	n/a
TOTAL	1.3	9.5	34.0	63

Source: RadioShack Company data.

also to give customers an opportunity to experience the home entertain-
ment capabilities of digital television, home theater, DVD players, and
RCA DirecTV satellite systems in a retail display custom designed for
RadioShack stores.

It is notable that Roberts and his team chose well-recognized branded
products as their anchors. They certainly had the option of private label
or new emerging brands that might provide better margins. But Roberts
tailored it to retain his focus on his customers. Branded products created
security for customers. Stocking branded products created a sense of pride
for employees; they could offer comparable products to the big box retailers and show customers how to connect them and use them effectively. For
Roberts and for employees, that strategy created an environment where
employees wanted to sell.

"BETTER AND BETTER ANSWERS"

In addition to providing new products for sale in the stores, RadioShack
provided extensive training for its sales associates on new products and
services. All of RadioShack's sales associates received the HOT training
program. Once again there was a reason for the HOT acronym. Len
Roberts had always believed that the purpose of communication was to
elicit action, and the more memorable and succinct the message, the better the chance of finding its target. As a senior manager at RadioShack
explained, "In this program, the 'H' is for helping the customer when
they come in for that part or accessory; the sales associate offers them the
'O', the opportunity to purchase another product or service; and then tells
(the 'T') the customers about the area that RadioShack wants to be famous
for, such as telecommunications."[11] RadioShack's telecommunications
strategy proved to be an outstanding success. In 1999, with sales of more
than $1 billion, the communications segment (that included wireless,
residential telephones, and other telephony products) overtook parts and
accessories as RadioShack's leading product category.

RadioShack's sales associates who were already superbly trained in
finding the appropriate part or accessory were provided further training to sell more complex products. The company used both traditional
and automated training techniques. Each sales associate was required
to be certified in particular product categories before being eligible
for promotion. Additionally, with the increased complexity of its business, RadioShack moved from a "retention" model, where employees
remembered all the relevant information, to a "retrieval" model, where
employees were taught how to retrieve information electronically on their
own. RadioShack also used its best salespeople to help train others in the
organization. For example, when RadioShack began selling long distance
services, it proved to be a difficult selling experience. As one executive

remarked, "We didn't have the right words."[12] So RadioShack brought its most successful salespeople to an offsite location to develop a sales process for use in all stores.

Roberts continued to demonstrate to the people of RadioShack that they were important. For example in 1998, Roberts turned from the products and stores to RadioShack's people, vowing to make RadioShack the "best company to work for in America." Roberts deeply believed that "before a store can be a great place to shop, it must first be a great place to work." To help define what a great place to work really meant, RadioShack created a task force of select employees and spouses to determine "the first initiatives for the Best Company movement." Based on a voting process, the task force decided on a short list of topics and then spent months researching and collecting employee's opinions. Specific recommendations were then forwarded to senior management. Changes resulting from the task force included the adoption of corporate values (teamwork, pride, trust, and integrity) and nine significant policy changes that included enhancement group insurance, a changed dress code, improved vacation policies, an upgrading of the new hire orientation programs, the development of a mentoring program, the introduction of flexible work hours, the provision of a family vacation planning service, and steps toward creating a positively motivated culture.

By 1999, RadioShack had become the largest retailer of wireless telephones, accounting for 70 percent of all wireless phones sold through noncarrier-owned retail outlets and 20 percent of all wireless phones sold. Wireless phones included both the Sprint PCS products and cellular products involving more than 40 cellular service partners. Another benefit of RadioShack's telecommunications strategy was the number of women that were brought into the stores. Customer research suggested that the focus on America's Telephone Store had helped shift the customer mix from 80 percent male/20 percent female to 68 percent male/32 percent female.

Once again, however, Roberts saw an opportunity for RadioShack to offer products and services at the forefront of technology. The Internet had exploded and the market appeared to be moving toward in-home broadband connections. As seen in Figure 11.3, Roberts believed that the next evolution for RadioShack would be to connect places, with RadioShack becoming America's Home Connectivity Store. To put his plan in motion, RadioShack acquired AmeriLink for $75 million to provide connectivity installation services. He envisioned as many as 10,000 RadioShack installation vans offering PC, satellite, and home-theater installations; high speed or broadband interest connections, and consumer electronics repairs and telecom systems upgrades. In November 1999, RadioShack signed a five-year agreement with Microsoft to develop a store-within-a-store, whereby customers could

Figure 11.3
(A) Parts and Accessories Anchor: Connecting "Things"; (B) Telecommunications Anchor: Connecting "People"; (C) Home Connectivity Anchor: Connecting "Places"

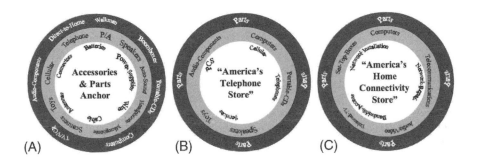

(A)   (B)   (C)

see demonstrations and sign up for Microsoft Network (MSN) dial-up or broadband Internet access

Ultimately, however, the Connecting Places strategy failed to come to fruition. This time RadioShack's timing was misaligned with the market.[13] In-home broadband did expand, but there were other challenges. RadioShack increasingly saw that the in-home connectivity strategy was outside of its core strengths—selling in-store and growing the customer sale by demonstrating and connecting the products right there in the store. By 2002, RadioShack exited the business.

The excitement in consumer electronics was about new technologies such as flat panel and plasma televisions. Unfortunately, these technologies required significant physical display space that was outside of RadioShack's small store capabilities. Rather than compete at a significant disadvantage, RadioShack opted to take a few years to improve the productivity of its supply chain and its stores. For the first time, RadioShack introduced standardized processes in its stores and completely revamped its supply chain and consolidated its store inventory systems. Several store-level product platforms were rationalized. Many processes were outsourced to vendors who brought better technology and efficiency to the operations. With all these changes, even though sales remained flat, margins rose.

Roberts knew that this internally focused work, although important and profitable, could last only one to two years; for while the RadioShack's store administrative function was part of these efforts, there was little

Figure 11.4
RadioShack—Communicating Strategy

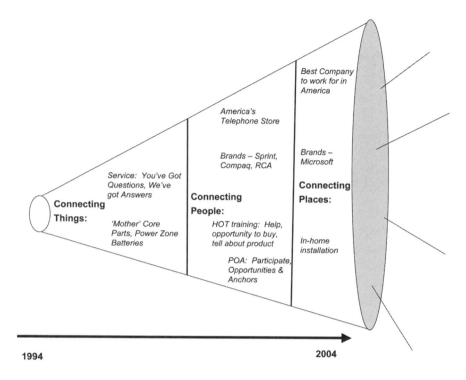

excitement and participation at the store level. According to Roberts, "Ultimately, people in the stores want to be 'part of the action' selling new products and solving new problems." On the telecommunications side they continued to do so, with photo-enhanced cell phones and the addition of Verizon as a carrier. But there was little in the way that they could contribute to systematic change. Roberts again recognized that a significant transformation was needed and in 2004 announced RadioShack's new strategic positioning that included the unveiling of a new retail store format, Concept 3, expansion into Canada, Mexico, and selected areas of the Caribbean, and new services businesses that leveraged RadioShack's retail coverage such as kiosk operations, wireless repairs, and distribution for new and emerging technologies. To help employees understand this strategy, Roberts positioned it as RadioShack's new solutions strategy—to dominate cost-effective solutions to meet everyone's routine electronic needs and families' distinct electronic wants.

In 2005, Len Roberts turned over the reins of his company to his longtime COO and partner at the top, Dave Edmondson. In keeping his position as Chairman, Roberts retained many of his ambassadorial functions, especially the outreach effort with employees. In each year of Roberts's 10 years at the helm of RadioShack, the revitalization strategy provided something new, different, and exciting for customers and employees. Some leaders create strategy and leave its communication and execution to others. Not so with Len Roberts, who used his strategy as a bullhorn (Figure 11.4) to embed it at two levels of the organization: the stores and the first level of management. He stayed with the message and communicated in a way that resonated with his people, fostering pride in their stores and their ability to serve customers. It was communicated in plain sales language that the salespeople in the store could understand and connect with. The message was the strategy, completely aligned all the way to the top of the organization. But then again Roberts did not rely solely on communication; he leveraged training and the organization to get the message hard wired into employees' day-to-day way of doing their work.

LESSONS LEARNED

In 1994, when Len Roberts first came to RadioShack, it was a business unit of Tandy Corporation. RadioShack's revenues were $2,853 million of Tandy's total revenues of $4,943 million. Net income for Tandy in 1994 was $224 million. Using the same proportion as sales, RadioShack's income was about $125 million. Net income for RadioShack in 2004 was $337 million. It would be reasonably accurate therefore to say that in the course of that decade, both sales and earnings grew at an average rate of about 6 to 8 percent, earnings, perhaps growing at a slightly higher rate. This, in an industry environment growing at less than 5 percent with significant store closures (such as Highland Appliance, Nobody Beats the Wiz, and 47th St. Photo), as well as changes in shopping habits where more than half of consumer electronics are purchased from superstores (Best Buy and Circuit City) and mass merchandisers (Wal-Mart and Target).

According to these parameters, Len Roberts's leadership of RadioShack has been successful and, as demonstrated in the preceding pages, his communications strategy has been a key component of that success. What can managers learn from RadioShack? Is this a strategy that leaders should replicate? If so, what are the ramifications of such a choice?

The first consideration is Len Roberts's choice of strategy. As indicated earlier, when Len Roberts came to RadioShack, he was faced with 7,000 small stores in a chain that many had thought was at best past its prime and at worst a dinosaur awaiting extinction. Roberts understood that he had to make RadioShack relevant again, but RadioShack's physical structure created constraints. Best Buy or Circuit City could create immediate impact with store redesign or new product assortment selections; within their big box format they had many merchandising options. RadioShack, however, with its 2,000 sq ft stores, was limited in product assortment options. Further, the company had just exited from an unsuccessful foray into a big box format so it was unlikely he could expand in that way; he had to work within the parameters of the small store format. Not having the flexibility to use a broader product assortment, or in-store merchandising, or store layout and ambience as a differentiating weapon, Len Roberts and his senior management team molded a service format that leveraged the company's convenient store locations and its core "parts" business. The way to animate this dimension of its strategy depended heavily on the involvement of front-line store personnel. That's what Len Roberts did. The communication style practiced by Len Roberts may not be that critical or crucial for all kinds of service businesses, only those where the strategy gets played out in a major way at the front line. Fortunately for RadioShack, not only was Len Roberts a great communicator, but he thoroughly enjoyed rubbing shoulders with his front-line employees.

Roberts successfully reached out to his people, but this approach isn't easy nor the challenges few. Leaders need to understand that this communications choice has implications; the communication needs to be continuous and the message needs to be compelling, requiring significant conscious effort on the part of the leader. Roberts varied his message, "connecting things, connecting people, connecting places," HOT program, "anchors." All the messages were designed to capture the attention of RadioShack's employees so that they acted out that message on the store floor. He tirelessly used multiple media: in person, satellite, video, and others. In some form, Len Roberts was there in the store with the sales person every day. Keeping the organization engaged, however, requires constant motivation. Engagement was high when cell phones and later when new branded products were introduced and even when core products such as batteries became the Power Zone. But when the strategy changed in 2002 to supply chain issues and cost containment in an effort to boost profits, it left the front-line employees without the pivotal role. The distribution and logistics arm of the company, operating centrally, took over. It was important for RadioShack to bring back its employees to a substantial role in carrying out the company's strategy. Its new CEO, Dave Edmondson, until his resignation in February 2006, had been working with his team on improving the company's profitability levels through "efficient supply chain." RadioShack's top management has since been working on multiple aspects of the firm's strategy, including what was previously considered untouchable – the store format, size, and layout.

In summary, the communications strategy that Len Roberts used so successfully at RadioShack is not for everyone. It requires effort, constant reinforcement, and continued engagement with the organization at its most basic levels. Even more fundamentally, its logic must fit the structure and strategy of the business. If the leader is the CEO, that chief executive must devote considerable time to make the strategy successful. This was the case at RadioShack.

NOTES

We thank Leonard Roberts, Radio Shack CEO 1994–2004, and Dave Edmondson, its COO from 2000–2004, and CEO since 2005, for their generosity and openness in sharing with us the several stages of RadioShack's strategy as described in this article. Much of the inferences made in this article are based on a Harvard Business School case study (#500–081) by V. Kasturi Rangan, Youngme Moon and Marie Bell.

1. Reporting to Len Roberts at that time were Dave Edmondson, COO; Francesca Spinelli, People; Evelyn Follit, CIO; Laura Moore Public Relations and Corporate Communications; Mark Hill, General Counsel; Dwain Hughes, CFO; and David Christopher, Tandy.

2. Laura Heller, "Radio Shack provides foundation for Tandy turnaround." *Discount Store News,* January 4, 1999.

3. Shoney's is a privately held family restaurant chain with about 300 franchised and company-owned outlets in the United States. Arby's is a leader in the beef sandwich segment of the restaurant business. It operated about 2,800 company-owned and franchised restaurants in the United States. Arby's restaurants varied in size from 700 to 4,000 sq ft

4. V. Rangan, Youngme Moon, and Marie Bell, "Radio Shack," Harvard Business School Case 500-081, 2000, 5.

5. Ibid., 10.

6. FoxNews, "RadioShack-CEO Interview, from FoxNews: Your World with Neil Cavuto," April 20, 2004.

7. Rangan, Moon, and Bell, "Radio Shack," 6.

8. Ibid., 11.

9. Ibid., 7.

10. Ibid., 8.

11. Ibid., 8.

12. Ibid., 10.

13. At the end of 2002, Best Buy, the leading consumer electronics retailer, announced its "Geek Squad": service teams located in store and capable of coming to customer's homes to solve electronics problems.

CHAPTER 12

Connecting with Employees through Front-Line Leadership: Lessons from Southwest Airlines

Jody Hoffer Gittell

The most influential leaders in our company—aside from Herb—are the front-line supervisors.
— Donna Conover, Executive Vice President of Customers, Southwest Airlines

Many front-line employees work in high-velocity settings, where operating conditions can change quickly, requiring employees to respond quickly. Popular belief holds that the best way to improve performance at the front lines in those settings is to create a "flat" organization in which there is little supervision, but where people are held to strict performance measures.

The "flat" organizational approach does appear attractive. In many cases, however, it does not live up to its potential to improve either the quality of jobs or the quality of service delivered to the customer. Strict systems of accountability tend to focus on narrow outcomes, which allow the company to maintain control, but in the process, undermine the kind of coordination that can allow a company to excel at service delivery.

It is better in these settings to build an organization based on cross-functional accountability, by enough supervisory staff to provide robust coaching and feedback. Put simply, the flat organizational approach, in practice, is less effective than having more supervisors managing smaller groups of employees, with performance measured across all the functions that are involved in a given work process.

When performance shortfalls are identified in an organization with functionally segregated performance measures at the front lines, employees are often quick to engage in finger pointing, which ultimately undermines teamwork and leaves problems unsolved. Cross-functional accountability, on the other hand, diffuses blame and encourages a system-wide approach to improvement. And the benefits of improved coordination that stem from having a smaller ratio of supervisors to front-line employees are significant.

Not that I advocate extreme micromanagement. But as seen later, having more supervisors with fewer people to supervise allows supervisors to actively coach and support front-line workers rather than to simply monitor their work. We'll also see that when only supervisors engage in coordination, the performance benefits are limited. The biggest benefits of increased supervisory staffing come when supervisors use their time to provide coaching and feedback to front-line employees, enabling front-line employees to coordinate their work *directly with each other*.

What's more, although this theory may seem at odds with quality improvement methodologies such as Six Sigma or TQM, it is not. Deming, the father of quality improvement, suggested that the *biggest obstacle to quality improvement is performance measurement systems that create fear by focusing on functional accountability rather than on the whole system*.[1] Cross-functional performance measures (supplemented by good coaching and feedback from managers) put the focus on the whole system and avoid the short-sighted approach that undermines coordination and learning.

The bottom line: performance measurement is important, but top managers who think that "flat" organizations are desirable should ask themselves what they might be giving up in return for that streamlined, tightly controlled structure. Much of my research has been in the airline and healthcare industries; however, in any turbulent operating environment, or any environment where employees need to respond to information that emerges from the work, coordination among front-line employees helps organizations achieve high performance outcomes. When front-line employees coordinate directly with each other, supported by their supervisors and not divided from each other by functionally specific performance measures, problems can be resolved on the spot, in a collaborative and timely way.

CONTROL AT THE EXPENSE OF COORDINATION

It's useful to explore in more detail the consequences of having a system of strict accountability in a flat organization. Much organizational literature has suggested that supervision should be replaced with systems of accountability and performance measurement. In flat organizations, the theory goes, with these systems in place employees can focus on the work itself and on their customers rather than on the chain of command.

The irony is that such systems of accountability and performance measurement, and the supposed "ideal" flat organizational structure, actually have unintended *negative* consequences. Supervisory coaching and feedback on the other hand have unexpected *positive* consequences.

The control gained by stepped up accountability and performance measurement can result in a group of employees concerned first with watching their own backs. They know that when mistakes occur, the company will try to place blame on an individual, or on an individual function, and they become protective of their "turf" and less open with employees in other functions, even when those functions together serve a single customer.

Increased supervision, on the other hand, in lieu of these very directed measurement systems, can result in a more trusting culture overall, with employees feeling freer to help one another solve problems, and also feeling that they can concentrate more fully on the service and performance goals of the *whole* team.

What's more, the supervisors with smaller spans of control are themselves freer to concentrate on the individuals who work under them, rather than on the "numbers" that those individuals generate. In the 1960s, management scholars found that supervisors with small spans of control were more available for coaching and feedback.[2] Managers with large spans had less opportunity for interacting with individual subordinates and maintaining effective relationships with them. They had less time to provide support, encouragement, and recognition to individual subordinates.[3] Managers with large spans were more likely to handle problems with subordinates in a more formalized, impersonal manner, using warnings and punishments instead of coaching and feedback. As spans of control increase, managers have been found to make more autocratic decisions.[4] Narrower spans of control have been found to allow more contact and more opportunities for communication between front-line and managerial employees.[5]

Note that nearly all these studies date from the 1960s. The tide has turned against supervision. Highly influential work by Richard Hackman and others has emphasized instead the intrusive nature of supervision and the need to replace supervisors with self-directed teams.[6] This work tends to overlook the positive potential of supportive front-line leadership and the negative consequences that arise when organizations replace personalized supervision with systems of accountability and performance measurement. More recently, management scholars have begun to discover again the importance of front-line leadership for both employee development and organizational performance.[7]

The bottom line is that front-line employees in organizations with more supervisors and less emphasis on systems of accountability benefit from more supervisory coaching and engage in more direct coordination with their fellow employees. Ultimately, customers benefit from the higher levels of quality and efficiency that are achieved through this approach.

OVEREXPOSED, UNDERTOLD: LESSONS FROM SOUTHWEST AIRLINES

The story of Southwest Airlines has been told many times in many different venues. It has been told so much, in fact, that the editor of this book requested that authors generally steer clear of Southwest and most other companies explored frequently in the media for fear that readers' eyes would glaze over at the names of these organizations, even if the authors did indeed have something new to say about them.

I've been granted an exception because important elements of the Southwest story remain underexposed, despite the company's phenomenal publicity, perhaps because these elements do not "fit" our common wisdom about how organizations should achieve high performance. Chief among those is that although Southwest Airlines is known as a flat, team-based company, it actually has more supervisors per front-line employee than any other major U.S. airline, with about 10 airport employees per front-line supervisor.

For managers in other organizations, the implications of this ratio, coupled with more broadly crafted systems of accountability and control, are significant. To illustrate that significance, we'll explore the Southwest approach to two common scenarios: (1) when mistakes occur and (2) when conflicts occur.

When Mistakes Occur at the Front Line

The flight departure process is one of the most complex processes that an airline must perform daily. Repeated hundreds of times daily in dozens of locations, its success or failure can make or break an airline's reputation for convenience and reliability. A departure is successful from the customer's point of view if it does not involve unnecessary hassles and if it results in the on-time arrival of the customer and his or her baggage. A departure is successful from the airline's point of view if these customer outcomes are achieved in an efficient way, without excess airport staffing or gate time for the airplane. Excess staffing carries obvious costs. Gate time is also costly because it represents time that the plane is sitting at the gate, not being used and not earning passenger revenues. Based on lost revenues alone, the cost of a hypothetical five-minute increase in gate time was estimated in the mid-1990s at $1.4 billion, or $4,120 per employee, for the 10 major U.S. airlines over a one-year period.

To achieve these performance goals, a multitude of tasks must be performed by groups with distinct skills under changing conditions in a limited period of time—between the arrival of a plane and its departure for the next flight. Pilots, flight attendants, gate agents, ticket agents, operations agents, mechanics, caterers, cabin cleaners, ramp agents, baggage handlers, cargo handlers, and fuelers all play significant roles (see Figure 12.1). Given high levels of uncertainty and time constraints, coordination among these groups is critical.

At many airlines, when a delay occurs, managers on duty are responsible for figuring out which function caused it. Immediate penalties accompany delays, in the form of having to explain what happened. Although the goal is to identify and fix problems quickly, the problem is that it often has the unintended effect of encouraging employees to look out for themselves and avoid recrimination, rather than focusing on their shared goals of on-time performance, accurate baggage handling, and satisfied customers. "If you ask anyone here, what's the last thing

Figure 12.1
The Flight Departure Process

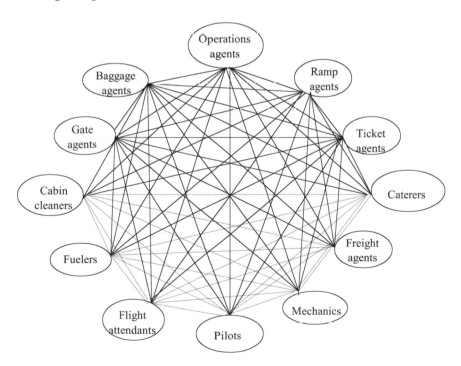

you think of when there's a problem," said one ramp supervisor at a Southwest competitor, "I bet your bottom dollar it's the customer. And these are guys who bust their butts everyday. But they're thinking, how do I keep my ass out of the sling."

Southwest's system, by contrast, diffuses blame and encourages employees faced with a problem or delay to continuously calibrate—as a team—their performance and focus on the customer.

Southwest uses a "team delay," which allows multiple functions to take responsibility for a particular delay. According to Jim Wimberly, executive vice president of operations, "We had too many angry disagreements between flight attendants and gate agents about whose delay it was. It was too hard to determine whose fault it was." One of Southwest's chief pilots explained, "The team delay is used to point out problems between two or three different employee groups in working together. We used to do it [in the following way]: if people were still in the jetway at departure time, it was a station delay. If people were on-board at departure time, it was a flight crew delay. But now if you see everybody working as a team, and it's a team problem, you call it a team delay. It's been a very positive thing."

The reduced precision of performance measurement did not appear to concern Southwest leaders. "We could have more delay categories," said Wimberly. "But we only end up chasing our tail."

When Conflicts Occur

At some airlines, conflict resolution is largely designed to address grievances between employees and managers, rather than conflicts among peers in different departments. In interviews, field managers claimed that resolving conflicts among employees was a relatively unimportant part of their jobs. Their performance evaluation system is based on results, they claimed, and it matters little to their rewards how those results were achieved. Although "supporting good working relationships" is included in their job descriptions, that item is allocated zero weight in the formal system of performance measurement used by headquarters.

At Southwest, by contrast, resolving conflicts between functional groups is addressed and valued explicitly. "What's unique about Southwest is that we're real proactive about conflict," said a field manager. "There is a lot of stress when the plane is on the ground," said Wimberly. "Inevitably some conflict will arise. All employees know, particularly operational employees, how things are supposed to go. If something happens out of the ordinary, if you feel someone didn't handle something correctly, you fill out a report."

"We are trying to push resolution of these conflicts and problems down to where they actually occur," Wimberly explained. "When the senior managers get the final report, we decide if a meeting is needed, if it looks like they haven't resolved it. We tell them this is not a disciplinary meeting . . . we'll leave the room if you like. We are just moderators; the focus is between employees and on how important teamwork is."

It is sometimes difficult to get employees together, for example if the conflict involves a pilot who is based in Baltimore and a gate agent who is based in Phoenix. Convening these sessions can also be intimidating, even for experienced managers. "You never know how it will turn out," said one. "Sometimes it blows up in your face." Still the results were usually worth the trouble, he said. According to SWA President Colleen Barrett, "it is wonderful to see the lights go off in people's eyes when they understand the other person's point of view."

A MORE PRODUCTIVE SUPERVISOR/
FRONT-LINE RATIO

At some airlines, as many as 40 front-line employees are "supervised" by one person. With this workload, supervisors reported they only had enough time to do their paperwork and to focus on the "bad apples," the problem employees, rather than provide coaching and support for all of them. Others reported they could stop by at the start of a shift to see that everyone was ready to go, but then would have little other interaction with their employees.

At Southwest, by contrast, one supervisor is responsible for approximately 10 front-line employees. Supervisors at Southwest told me that the people who reported to them were their internal customers and that their job was to help these people do their jobs better. "We are responsible for what the agents do," explained one supervisor. "It is very difficult sometimes, because it's such a family-oriented company. You might feel like a sister to one of the [front-line workers], then you have to bring discipline. You have to step back and put the friendship aside and say, 'I don't agree with what you just did.' But the [front-line workers] are also our customers. We are here to help them do their jobs."

The supervisory role at Southwest was not primarily to monitor front-line employees: "If there is a problem like one person taking a three-hour lunch, they take care of that themselves for the most part. Peer pressure works well." In addition, supervision was not just about telling people what to do: "You could just point to this and that. But you don't have to—everybody knows what to do."

The supervisor's role was primarily to facilitate learning. "I would be personally offended if their only drive was that if the plane didn't leave on time, they'd come in to my office to—you know, the threats," said a station manager. "I don't feel they're afraid of me and that means a lot. If there's a delay, we find out why it happened. We get ideas from them on how to do it better next time. If you've got that kind of relationship then they're not going to be afraid.

"Say there was a 10-minute delay because freight was excessive. If I'm screaming I won't know why it was late. They'll think, 'He's an idiot, if only he knew.' Then they'll start leaving stuff behind or they'll just shove it in, and I won't know. If we ask, 'Hey what happened?' then the next day the problem is taken care of. We move the freight, we re-route the freight to where it's less damaging. You have to be in that mode every day. There's no one person who can do it. We all succeed together—and all fail together. You have to truly live it."

BOTTOM LINE

The two alternative control systems we've discussed are summarized in Table 12.1. One column represents Southwest's approach; the other represents a competitor's. Both are internally consistent and self-reinforcing, but one appears to be more effective than the other. One system achieves control through functional accountability, measuring performance "by the numbers" and assigning outcomes to individual departments. Because control in such an organization is based on objective performance evaluation, which can be carried out from a distance, supervisory functions can be minimized. Such an organization therefore can become quite flat in the field operation. Systems of functional accountability thus achieve control in a fairly efficient way, but systems of functional accountability tend to produce weak coordination. Control is achieved in a way that undermines rather than supports coordination.

Table 12.1
Alternative Systems for Achieving Coordination and Control

	American	Southwest
Control Mechanisms	Functional accountability	Cross-functional accountability
	Large supervisory span of control	Small supervisory span of control
Human Resource Practices	Selection for functional skills	Selection for cross-functional teamwork
	Minimal cross-functional conflict resolution	Proactive cross-functional conflict resolution

Southwest's system, by contrast, was premised on the need for coordination. Over time Southwest's leaders developed a way to achieve control without undermining coordination. They created the concept of a "team delay" that reduced the precision of performance measurement to reduce unproductive blaming. They staffed supervisory positions adequately to allow supervisors to play a coaching role, reinforcing a focus on learning, and allowing for richer communication across levels of the organization than could be captured by "the numbers" alone. Likewise in the relationship between headquarters and the field, they took the approach of active feedback delivered in a nonpunitive way, resulting in richer two-way communication than could be captured by quantitative measures alone. To further support this system of cross-functional accountability, they hired people based on their potential for engaging in cross-functional teamwork. They established a process to resolve conflicts between the functions and to build a common understanding of the departure process.

With fewer direct reports, Southwest supervisors also had greater opportunities for working side by side with the front-line employees they were responsible for supervising. Working together appeared to reduce informational and social distance between supervisors and the supervised, and to support the creation of shared goals. Shared goals in turn made front-line employees more receptive to supervisory coaching and feedback, and reduced the role of supervisory monitoring even further as employees began to monitor each other. With fewer social and informational boundaries between themselves and their direct reports, supervisors were able to perform their coaching and feedback functions more effectively.

The other airline's system allowed it to operate with a relatively low level of trust: indeed it is virtually guaranteed to produce low trust by setting up conflicts over who is responsible for problems. But in areas that require high levels of coordination, like the flight departure process, it is less effective than the alternative. Southwest's system is conducive to coordination of flight departures, but it is far more vulnerable to the loss of trust. Employees are not as easily evaluated and motivated according to clearly delineated functional goals. Good performance is not so easily defined. Often, it is "doing whatever is needed to get the job done." Such performance goals cannot be measured easily "by the numbers." More fine-tuned evaluation is needed. The Southwest model achieves control instead through practices that emphasize the rich flow of information up and down the organization. The span of control, or number of employees per supervisor, is much smaller to allow a more fine-tuned interaction between supervisors and front-line employees.

These two cases suggest several propositions for achieving control in a way that supports rather than undermines coordination; these are presented in Table 12.2.

Southwest chose to increase supervision and to reduce the emphasis on performance measurement by adopting cross-functional accountability. These choices were mutually reinforcing. With a system of performance measurement that offered less detailed information about performance, more supervisors were needed for coaching and feedback. Both of these choices were also conducive to coordination. Cross-functional accountability increased cooperation and learning across functional boundaries by taking the focus off of finger-pointing and reducing the fear factor,

Table 12.2
Propositions

Control Mechanisms	Cross-functional Accountability	Shared accountability across functional lines diffuses blame and finger-pointing, encourages shared goals, and improves quality and efficiency performance.
	Supervisory Span of Control	Small supervisory spans of control allow coaching and feedback across levels of the organization, improving shared goals and shared knowledge among employees, as well as quality and efficiency performance.
Human Resource Practices	Selection for Teamwork	Selecting for teamwork identifies people who will treat their counterparts in other functions with respect, and who will take responsibility for outcomes beyond their own functions, improving both quality and efficiency performance.
	Cross-functional Conflict Resolution	Cross-functional conflict resolution resolves misunderstandings as they emerge, and creates a better shared understanding of the overall process and its participants, improving both quality and efficiency performance.

and narrow spans of control allowed supervisors to engage actively in supporting coordination through coaching and feedback.

Table 12.3 shows that higher staffing levels for supervisors generate more coordination by supervisors *and* more coordination by front-line employees themselves. We can also see that both kinds of coordination are beneficial for the organization and its customers. Table 12.4 shows that increased coordination by supervisors themselves leads to substantial performance benefits. But increased coordination by front-line employees leads to even greater performance benefits.

The bottom line is that supervisors play a critical role, but it's not just their direct involvement in coordination that helps. Rather, supervisors have their biggest impact by supporting front-line employees' efforts to coordinate *directly with each other.*

Table 12.3
Impact of Supervisory Staffing on Coordination*

	Coordination by Supervisors	Coordination by Front-Line Employees
Supervisory	.36**	.45***
Staffing	(.009)	(.000)
Flights/Day	−.40**	−.33***
	(.003)	(.000)
Gate Agent	.15	.34***
	(.321)	(.000)
Baggage Agent	.06	.13*
	(.645)	(.030)
Ramp Agent	.48**	.34***
	(.003)	(.000)
Operations Agent	.37*	.41***
	(.012)	(.000)
R^2	0.36	0.29

*Supervisory staffing is measured as the number of supervisors per hundred frontline employees. Coordination, defined as coordinating work through shared goals, shared knowledge and mutual respect, is measured as the percent of cross-functional ties that are "strong" or "very strong" based on an employee survey. Both models are random effects regressions with employee as the unit of analysis (n = 301 front-line employees and n = 53 supervisory employees) and site (n = 9) as the random effect. Statistical significance is denoted: *$p<0.05$, **$p<0.01$, ***$p<0.001$, and suggests the certainty that a change in supervisory staffing will produce a change in coordination, where a smaller p value suggests a higher certainty. R^2 denotes the percentage of the variation in coordination that is explained by the model.

Table 12.4
Performance Effects of Coordination by Supervisors vs. Front-Line Employees[*]

	Quality Performance	Efficiency Performance
Coordination by Supervisors	.73*** (.001)	.33*** (.000)
Coordination by Front-Line Employees	1.12*** (.000)	.54*** (.000)
Flights/Day	.10 (.301)	.26*** (.000)
Flight Length, Passengers and Cargo per Flight	1.04*** (.000)	−.23*** (.015)
Passenger Connections	.75** (.001)	.22 (.011)
R^2	0.49	0.92

[*]Quality performance includes customer complaints, mishandled bags, and late arrivals, combined into an equally weighted index and reverse-coded. Efficiency performance includes aircraft turnaround time per departure and staff time per passenger, combined into an equally weighted index and reverse-coded. Coordination, defined as coordinating work through shared goals, shared knowledge, and mutual respect is measured as the percent of cross-functional ties that are "strong" or "very strong" based on an employee survey. Both models are random effects regressions with site/month as the unit of analysis (n = 99) and site (n = 9) as the random effect. Statistical significance is denoted: *$p<0.05$, **$p<0.01$, ***$p<0.001$ and suggests the certainty that a change in coordination will produce a change in performance, where a smaller p value suggests a higher certainty. R^2 denotes the percentage of the variation in performance that is explained by the model.

OTHER CRITICAL FACTORS

Only a small part of the Southwest story is told here. Many other important factors contribute to the overall success of the airline and the well-being of the front-line crews, and excluding these factors from this discussion would be misleading. The Southwest approach described here is not a silver bullet; it is one important element among several that result in the recipe that makes Southwest successful. What's more, Southwest's competitive strategy lends itself to this approach.

Other airlines, for example, might have developed a weaker capability for coordination because their strategies are fundamentally different from that of Southwest. Being a hub-and-spoke carrier, rather than a point-to-point carrier, for example, might make quick turnarounds arguably less relevant. Competitors' hubs might generate pricing power that counterbalances the inherent costs of the hub-and-spoke system. According to one senior vice president of planning, a hub can generate up to 20 percent more revenue per plane than a comparable point-to-point flight.

Southwest, on the other hand, as a point-to-point carrier, has neither hubs nor pricing power. Southwest instead uses a quick turnaround strategy, and the high aircraft utilization inherent in this strategy, to offer low cost air travel to consumers. The quick turnaround strategy requires a simple product and a configuration of assets—aircraft, routes and maintenance facilities—that is different from that of a hub-and-spoke operation, and it clearly requires high levels of coordination. Now that the pricing power of hubs is in jeopardy because of the rise of point-to-point airlines such as Southwest, even airlines with major hubs are seeking to turn their planes faster, so coordination is becoming more relevant for them, too.

Southwest also has an in-depth hiring process, with tight screens for people with the type of work ethic and general attitude toward colleagues that the airline desires. We have not covered that process in this chapter, but it is clearly a contributing factor to the success of the airline's approach to front-line employee management. Front-line employees can cover a wide range of functional expertise, from mechanics to pilots to flight attendants; Southwest deliberately screens for people who will work well with colleagues across this range.

QUESTIONS TO ASK IF YOU CONSIDER THIS APPROACH

- Have we reduced the number of front-line supervisors in our company over the past decade to cut costs or to achieve a more responsive organization?
- Were the expected outcomes achieved?
- How has the increased span of control affected the ability of supervisors to coach and support employees?
- Is there a unit or section of our company where we could launch an experiment to expand the number of front-line supervisors, to get a span of control closer to 10? If there is and the plan is to conduct the experiment, first measure overall employee satisfaction and employee satisfaction with supervisory support, as well as operational performance (quality and efficiency) in the unit selected. Increase supervisory staffing, then measure these same variables again six months later. Be sure to select and train your new supervisors, not only for their skill in doing the work that they will be supervising, but also for their "relational competence."

For more on this topic, see Chapters 6 and 7 of *The Southwest Airlines Way: Using the Power of Relationships to Achieve High Performance.*

For purposes here, it is sufficient to highlight the potentially significant upsides to enhanced supervision, and redefined performance measurement systems. For many companies, this is a new concept, and implementation would require a shift in mindset regarding organizational structure and a corresponding shift in resource allocation.

NOTES

This chapter adapts and builds upon material from Jody Hoffer Gittell's book, *The Southwest Way: Using the Power of Relationships to Achieve High Performance* (New York: McGraw-Hill 2003) and also from her articles, "Paradox of Coordination and Control" *California Management Review* 42(3) (January 2000): 177–183 (Copyright © 2000, by The Regents of the University of California. Reprinted from the *California Management Review,* Vol. 42, No. 3. By permission of The Regents.) and "Supervisory Span, Relational Coordination and Flight Departure Performance: A Reassessment of Post-Bureaucracy Theory" *Organization Science* 12(4)(August 2001): 467–482. All quotations in this chapter are from these works.

1. J.E. Deming, *Out of the Crisis* (Cambridge, Mass.: MIT Press, 1986).
2. L. Porter and E. Lawler, "The Effects of 'Tall' versus 'Flat' Organization Structures on Managerial Job Satisfaction," *Personnel Psychology* 17 (1964): 135–148.
3. J.D. Ford "Department Context and Formal Structure as Constraints on Leader Behavior," *Academy of Management Journal* 24 (1981): 274–288; B.E. Goodstadt and D. Kipnis, "Situational Influences on the Use of Power," *Journal of Applied Psychology* 54 (1970): 201–207.
4. D. Kipnis and J. Cosentino, "Use of Leadership Powers in Industry," *Journal of Applied Psychology* (1969) 53: 460–466; D. Kipnis, D. W. P. Lane, "Self-Confidence and Leadership," *Journal of Applied Psychology* 46 (1962): 291–295; F. Heller and G. Yukl "Participation, Managerial Decision-Making and Situational Variables," *Organizational Behavior and Human Performance* 4 (1969): 227–241.
5. L. Porter and E. Lawler (1964), "The Effects of 'Tall' versus 'Flat' Organization Structures on Managerial Job Satisfaction," *Personnel Psychology,* (1968) 135–148; P. Blau "The Hierarchy of Authority in Organizations," *American Journal of Sociology* (1968): 453–467.
6. R. Hackman and G. Oldham *Work Redesign* (New York: Addison-Wesley, 1980); R. Walton and R. Hackman, "Groups Under Contrasting Management Strategies," in *Designing Effective Work Groups,* eds. P. Goodman and Associates. (San Francisco: Jossey-Bass, 1986); Eileen Appelbaum and Rosemary Batt, *The New American Workplace* (Ithaca, N.Y.: ILR Press, 1994); Charles Heckscher and Anne Donnellon, eds., *The Post-Bureaucratic Organization: New Perspectives on Organizational Change* (Thousand Oaks, Calif.: Sage, 1994); S. Zuboff, *In the Age of the Smart Machine: The Future of Work and Power* (New York: Basic Books, 1988).

7. M. Higgins and D.A. Thomas, "Constellations and Careers: Toward Understanding the Effects of Multiple Developmental Relationships," *Journal of Organizational Behavior* 22(3) (2001): 223–247; M. Bokeno and V.W. Gantt, "Dialogic Mentoring: Core Relationships for Organizational Learning," *Management Communication Quarterly* 14(2) (2000): 237–270; A.D. Ellinger and R.P. Bostrom, "Managerial Coaching Behaviors in Learning Organizations," *Journal of Management Development,* 18(9) (1999): 752.

PART IV

History Tells Us ...

Sometimes it takes an old story to spark new thinking . . .

CHAPTER 13

Great Leaders Create Environments That Unlock Potential and Lift the Human Spirit

Michael Lee Stallard, Carolyn Dewing-Hommes, and Jason Pankau

In 490 B.C., Darius, king of the Persian Empire, sent 26,000 soldiers to conquer the city-state of Athens.[1] Although Athens was insignificant in size compared to the vast Persian Empire, the Athenians decided to fight rather than surrender their way of life. Their decision looked like suicide. The Athenian citizen-soldiers were outarmed and outnumbered nearly three-to-one. What's more, the Persians were a war machine; the Athenians were a comparatively peaceful people.

Yet on the plain of Marathon, Greece, the Athenian citizen-soldiers pulled off one of the greatest upsets of all time. They defeated a Persian army that hadn't lost a battle in decades. What led them to victory? Probably a whole host of factors. But the father of history, Herodotus, and the Greek playwright Aeschylus, both writing about the battle, identified the Athenians' love of freedom as one of the reasons they were motivated to defeat the Persians.

Unlike the Athenians, all Persians beneath King Darius were viewed as his servants. Darius made the decisions and everyone else followed them. In contrast, Athenian citizens felt a sense of personal value, they shared a common vision for a free society, and they had a voice in the decision-making process of their city-state. They knew Athenian life was better than life under Darius, and they were willing to die if necessary to live in the environment that they favored.

A decade after the Persian defeat in the battle of Marathon, Darius's son, King Xerxes, sent more than a 100,000 soldiers in 1,207 ships back to Athens to attack them in what became known as the Battle of Salamis.

Although the Athenians and some of their fellow city-states likely had a tenth of the soldiers and less than one-third of the ships that Persia had, the Greeks prevailed again. After the defeat, Xerxes sent an offer of peace to the Athenians. Their reply: *never!*

The Athenian victories against the Persians provide an important lesson for leaders: *the environment people live and/or work in is key to achieving and sustaining their peak performance.* It's true whether you lead a nation, a business, or a basketball team. And creating an engaging work environment is as necessary today as it was in ancient Athens.

Great leaders throughout history have learned that the environment you establish makes a difference. It helped a 25-year old Queen Elizabeth I in 1558 transform a bankrupt England into one of the most powerful nations on earth over the course of her four-plus decade reign. It helped General George Washington lead a ragtag, under equipped colonial army to defeat England, the greatest military power at the time, during the American Revolution. Subsequently, an engaging environment helped the young nation rise, within 50 years beginning in 1760, as historian Gordon Wood stated in his Pulitzer-prize winning book, *The Radicalism of The American Revolution:*

[from] less than two million monarchical subjects ... on the very edges of the civilized world . . . to a giant, almost continent-wide republic of nearly ten million egalitarian-minded bustling citizens who not only had thrust themselves into the vanguard of history but had fundamentally altered their society and their social relationships. . . . Americans had become, almost overnight, the most [free], the most democratic, the most commercially minded, and the most modern people in the world.[2]

More recently, an engaging environment helped transform a competitive Chicago Bulls team into a basketball dynasty, an unassuming Detroit Piston basketball team into NBA champions, and a low-key New England Patriots football team into the NFL champions three of the last four years. It also contributed to stunning turnarounds at Procter and Gamble, Apple Computer, and The Xerox Corporation.

No doubt, again, a host of factors were at work in each of these cases. But reduced to their essentials, what can these success stories tell us?

Task Excellence + Engaging Work Environment = Sustainable Superior Performance

In their pursuit of positive business results, most organizations today have become masters of "task excellence," that is, the "hard," mechanical, and analytically oriented aspects of business implicit in such areas as Six Sigma, benchmarking, and performance measurement metrics. There's no question that task excellence is necessary; it's just not enough. With task excellence alone, success is fleeting. Leaders may get their people to perform well for a period of time, but eventually, without engagement, their energy will dissipate.

Only when leaders motivate people by creating an engaging work environment do they realize the energy, optimism, trust, cooperation, innovation, and productivity necessary to produce the *sustainable* peak performance of people. Unfortunately, few organizations have mastered engaging the people who work for them.

We came to this conclusion after completing a multiyear research project to understand what motivates people at work. As part of the project we conducted interviews with employees and employers, reviewed existing research, and consulted with experts in psychology, organizational behavior, sociology, and neuroscience. In the end, we concluded that the key to motivating people for long periods is to put into place the five elements that create an engaging work environment.

An engaging work environment provides the lubrication, if you will, to make the machinery of task excellence and superior performance sustainable. Engagement not only improves employee motivation, it also naturally enhances working relationships and has a positive impact on innovation and productivity. With an engaging work environment leaders discover a new means to improve customer satisfaction and a new source of sustainable competitive advantage.

What does it take to motivate people and engage them? Money, power, and fame have long been the "carrots" of motivation. Certainly, they motivate people. The problem is that in most organizations there's not enough of each commodity to motivate more than a few top employees, and it only motivates them up to a point. When you want to motivate people at all levels of your organization, money, power, and fame alone are not viable solutions.

When we speak of creating an engaging environment we are not advocating having employees standing around, holding hands, and singing "Kumbayah." We are not promoting having a wimpy work environment or holding group therapy sessions. We know that you may not like all of the people you work with. That said, it is possible to create a work environment that brings out the best in people and cultivates healthy working relationships. An engaging environment is common sense yet uncommon in practice. In most organizations there is a gap between what exists today and the work environment we all long for. Wise leaders are beginning to see this and do something about it.

In this chapter, we examine each of the five elements of an engaging work environment by looking at stories of how leaders did or did not employ each one. We will also provide a few suggestions on how to bring these elements to your work environment. Figure 13.1 is a visual representation of the five elements.

Figure 13.1
The Engaging Work Environment

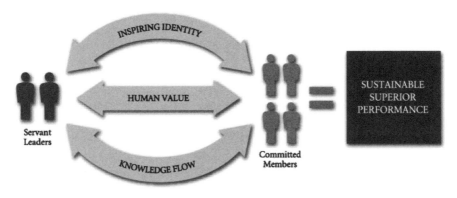

ELEMENT 1: HUMAN VALUE

The first element of an engaging environment is evident in the story of an eighteenth-century Prussian Prince, Frederick II.[3] As a young man, Prince Frederick was in an unbearable situation. Residing in the capitol of Berlin, Frederick longed for autonomy and independence but lived under a cruel and autocratic father, Frederick I, the first King of Prussia. The king disapproved of Fredrick's more modern ways, so he beat and berated him publicly to force his son to comply with his wishes.

When the prince was 18 years old, he and a friend were apprehended trying to escape to England. For his punishment, the king made Frederick watch as his friend was beheaded. Out of these harsh experiences Frederick learned what it felt like to be on the receiving end of a ruler who wielded power to force people to obey him. Unfortunately, at the time, there was nothing young Frederick could do about it. So he patiently waited for his hour to arrive.

In 1740, after the death of his father, Frederick II assumed the Prussian throne. He was determined to lead in a far different way than his father had. Influenced by the writings of John Locke and the Roman orator Cicero, Frederick described himself as "the first servant of the state" and used his power to improve the lives of the Prussian people. He lived in modest accommodations rather than pretend he was some demigod deserving of an enormously extravagant lifestyle like the Bourbon kings of France whose opulence fueled popular outrage and contributed to the French Revolution.

The results of Frederick's rule were extraordinary. Instead of acting like a dictator, Frederick established freedom of the press and a policy of religious toleration. He established individual protections under law by expediting the legal process and abolishing torture. He educated judges, leading the Prussian courts to gain the reputation as being the fairest courts in Europe. He rebuilt towns and roads to connect communities. He promoted education for his people. During the Seven Years' War he successfully defended Prussia from French, Russian, and Austrian attacks despite having fewer military resources. Ultimately, he built Prussia into one of the strongest states in Europe.

Historian James McGregor Burns called him "one of the most masterful . . . constructive and successful rulers in recent times." Voltaire, the French philosopher, described Frederick as "the Philosopher King." But it was his people who called him the name by which he will forever be remembered: Frederick the Great. By removing some of the elements in the Prussian environment that devalued people and adding elements that enhanced human value, Frederick helped the Prussian people realize more of their potential.

Frederick realized great success early in his reign, but later on he began to fail as a leader. His insatiable desire for military conquest to achieve personal fame and meet his dead father's expectations overcame his desire to help the people. Eventually, the bloody battles Frederick undertook, along with sleeplessness and nightmares he had about his father, contributed to poor health and his growing sense of hopelessness and despair. As he aged, Frederick's behavior toward others became abusive. Although he had at one time won the devotion of the Prussian people, at the time of his death in 1786 few mourned him.

From eighteenth-century Prussia let's go to the mid-1970s where we will look at a leader in a corporate setting who added elements to the environment that enhanced the value of people.

The preeminent management sage, the late Peter Drucker knew some of the greatest leaders of our times in business and government. If he had named the person he thought was or is a model leader, would he have chosen President Dwight D. Eisenhower, General George C. Marshall, the legendary Alfred P Sloan Jr. of General Motors, or one of the many other heads of major companies throughout the world he had come to know over his distinguished career? It's an interesting question, given Drucker's reach and influence. Periodically in his interviews and writings you will encounter what may be his highest praise for a person who he once remarked "could manage any company in America."[4] Who is she? *Business Week* featured her on its cover surrounded by . . . Girl Scouts. Her name is Frances Hesselbein.

Although she had no daughters, Mrs. Hesselbein began her association with the Girl Scouts when she agreed to help with a troop of 30 Girl

Scouts in Johnstown, Pennsylvania, who had lost their leader. It wasn't long before Frances Hesselbein's experience with Troop 17 developed into a lifelong commitment to Girl Scouting. Years later she would become CEO of the national organization, Girl Scouts of the U.S.A.

Mrs. Hesselbein's leadership style, in fact it seems her purpose in life, is to bring out the best in the people she meets along life's journey. Her words and actions evoke a high regard for people. Mrs. Hesselbein has written that good leaders have an "appreciation of their colleagues individually and the dignity of the work their colleagues do." Her actions show that she "walks the talk." Mrs. Hesselbein approaches communication in an inclusive way, expanding information out in ever-larger circles across the organization. Rather than lecturing, she asks insightful questions to draw out relevant issues. In planning and allocating the Girl Scout organization's resources, she introduced a circular management process that involved virtually everyone across the organization. Always caring, she sees the best in people.

With Frances Hesselbein as its leader, the Girl Scout organization thrived. When she assumed the CEO position in 1976, the Girl Scout's membership was declining and the organization was in a state of serious decline. She put sound management practices in place. She developed people. On her watch she built a conference center to train Girl Scout staff. The result was that during her 24-year tenure, Girl Scout membership quadrupled to nearly 3.5 million, diversity more than tripled, and the organization was transformed into what Drucker called "the best-managed organization around." Hesselbein accomplished the amazing transformation with an employed staff of 6,000 and 780,000 volunteers.

By the time Hesselbein resigned from the Girl Scouts in 1990, the organization's future was bright. She was paid the ultimate complement by Drucker when he recruited her to be the head of The Drucker Foundation (renamed the Leader to Leader Institute), which is dedicated to carrying out their mutual passion for strengthening leadership in the social sector. It should be no surprise that the foundation's influence is rapidly growing worldwide with Hesselbein leading the effort. After all, Peter Drucker knew a great leader when he saw one.

In her words and actions, Frances Hesselbein expanded what we describe as *human value*, the first of the five elements in an engaging environment. Frederick the Great and the Prussian people also benefited from human value until Frederick became obsessed with power. We define the element of human value as follows:

When everyone in the organization operates with an understanding of the universal nature of people, appreciates the positive, unique contributions of each of their colleagues, and strives to help them achieve their potential.

Human value means that leaders remove elements in the work environment that devalue people and add elements that increase their value. A work environment where human value is present brings out the best in people by affirming them, and giving them hope and a reason to be optimistic about their future. Here are a few practical ways that every leader can increase human value in the work environment.

1. *Make a human connection with as many people as possible.* Leaders need to acknowledge individuals. That's why emotionally intelligent leaders make it a point to know the names of many people in their organizations. Learning people's personal stories, especially those people with whom you regularly work, also is much appreciated. Try to remember something about the people you lead whether it's their hobby or favorite sports team. For the leader who leads large numbers of people, human connections can be made by simple acts such as meeting them, maintaining eye contact, saying something to them as you pass in the hallway, and acknowledging what they say to you.

2. *Treat and speak to employees as partners.* Treat people across the organization's hierarchy as equals. This shows that you value them. Confidence is to be encouraged, but arrogance and condescension are not. Patronizing behavior devalues others and poisons the environment. Treat everyone with respect to promote an egalitarian atmosphere. For example, choose job titles that reflect equality among all employees, such as the "partners" at Starbucks or "crew members" at JetBlue Airlines.[5] It's a small but significant gesture to show human value.

3. *Get rid of leaders who are uncivil to others.* No one should be in a leadership position who regularly treats people in an uncivil way. Make certain leaders know that it is impermissible for anyone (whether directed at an individual or group of people) to yell, scream, curse, intentionally ignore, constantly interrupt, violate someone's personal space, intimidate, belittle, or condescend. This behavior devalues people and thereby reduces trust and cooperation between employees and their leaders.

4. *Help employees find the right positions.* You will reap tremendous benefits if you help people better understand their values, abilities, and temperaments and find positions that fit who they are. A person in the wrong role is likely to feel disengaged. That person will be stressed out if overly challenged and bored if unchallenged. Supervisors or mentors can often better assess someone's talents than the person can. The assessment process also opens people's eyes to how different we all are in our unique blend of talents, temperaments, and learning and thinking styles. Assessment tools are available to help individuals do this. Unfortunately, few companies or leaders provide this type of assistance to all their employees.

5. *Decentralize decision making and eliminate unnecessary rules.* Allow people to make their own decisions. This shows them you respect their abilities and judgment, and that you value them. Many firms have decentralized decision making. They've learned from experience that decentralized decision making improves morale by providing a greater sense of control to lower level employees. Also, eliminate unnecessary rules. Rules are another form of control and excessive

rules do more damage than good. Unless a rule is absolutely necessary, get rid of it or make it a guideline.

6. *Recognize the human need for balance.* We all have times in life when things outside of work require more of our attention. Often it's the health of a loved one or our own health. Leaders need to balance giving people time off to attend to urgent needs in their personal lives and the need to be fair to other employees who have to do more of the work when one of their colleagues is away. Unless the situation of the employee in need requires privacy, and with the person's permission, communicate to the group why it is necessary to help one of their own.

7. *Inform people, seek their views and consider them.* Give people input in the decision-making process. This will also help engage them. We'll discuss this in more detail when we look at the element of *knowledge flow.*

Great leaders know the foundation of a successful human enterprise is human value. Frederick the Great established greater freedom and opportunity for his people; Frances Hesselbein cared for her people, was positive and encouraging, and sought their opinions and then considered them. Enhancing human value in the environment is one reason leaders such as Fredrick the Great and Frances Hesselbein inspired people, won their admiration, and brought out their best efforts.

ELEMENT 2: INSPIRING IDENTITY

The second element of an engaging environment was used by the leader who most historians cite as among the best American presidents in history: Franklin Delano Roosevelt (FDR).[6] Thanks in part to his inspiring leadership, the American people survived the Depression and, as part of the Allies, achieved victory in World War II.

One of the key events that helped the Allies prevail was the productivity of American workers. To speed up production, FDR made it a priority to visit plants and shipyards and motivate workers. On one such occasion while speaking to 18,000 workers at a Boeing aircraft plant near Seattle, FDR brought along with him Hewitt Wheless, an American pilot whose plane had been shot over the Pacific Ocean and yet was able to fly out of harm's way. When the workers saw the decorated pilot and heard him tell the story of how the B-17 plane built at their plant saved his life, you can bet they swelled with pride. Welding joints and tightening screws were transformed from mundane tasks into important work to win the war and protect some family's loved one. FDR helped transform the way they thought of themselves from aircraft factory workers to defenders of freedom. He told an inspiring story that instilled a sense of pride and purpose in the hearts and minds of workers on the home front. And they delivered. From 1941 until 1945, American aircraft manufacturers responded by out-producing German manufacturers at a rate of nearly three-to-one. During those five years they produced nearly 300,000 airplanes![7]

Decades later, in the San Francisco Bay area, Steve Jobs did something similar to help resurrect the company he had co-founded in his garage back in 1976. After a 12-year exile from Apple, Jobs initially returned as an advisor in late 1996 and then was made interim CEO in 1997.[8] Beginning in January 2000, he assumed the lead as Apple's CEO. Before Jobs's return, Apple's future looked dismal. Its performance had slipped and it was rumored to be an acquisition target.

A critical juncture in Apple's revival occurred in the fall of 1997, when Steve Jobs met with Apple's advertising agency, Chiat/Day, to consider ideas for a new advertising campaign. The agency presented the "Think Different" concept and Jobs loved it. The ads described not just Apple's customers but its employees as well. It also described how Steve Jobs liked to think of himself. After giving the ad agency the go-ahead, Jobs worked closely with the agency's creative people to develop television spots that featured black-and-white photos of people who changed the world through their creativity: people such as Albert Einstein, Mahatma Gandhi, and Pablo Picasso.

At a gathering with Apple employees, Steve Jobs introduced the campaign. They loved it, too. It was bold, visually striking, and, most of all, inspiring. It would tell the world what Apple stood for and, by implication, something about the people who worked there: they are creative, driven to innovate, and thereby help change the world. Also contributing to Apple's identity was the aesthetic appeal of its advertising and product design that communicated that employees of Apple are artists as much as they are engineers.

Within a few months of launching the "Think Different" campaign, Apple began hitting its financial targets as it experienced increased sales of its Macintosh computers. Not surprisingly, employee turnover fell. Today Apple continues to build on the message with its award winning I-Pod advertising. Apple's cachet, brand, attraction to employees, financial results, and future have never looked better.

FDR and Steve Jobs knew that people are more engaged when they are *inspired* and through their inspiration find meaning in their work. The second element in an engaging environment is *inspiring identity*. We define it as follows:

When everyone in the organization is united and motivated by a clear understanding of who "we" are as a company, what we stand for, how we are different, where we are going, how we are going to get there, why it is important, and how each of us fits in.[9]

Everyone has a sense of identity. It's how we think about ourselves and is shaped by where we were born, how we were raised, and by the people and events in our lives that influenced our beliefs and our aspirations. We like to think of identity as an individual's *story*. Haven't you been inspired by knowing the stories of others? Haven't you found that knowing someone's story gave you insight into her behavior or his viewpoint?

Organizations have stories, too. Unfortunately, most leaders miss the importance of this fact. They fail to impart an inspiring identity because, in typical *task* fashion, they compose a mission statement and think they are finished. Not counting the Human Resources department, how many people in your organization are even able to recall the mission statement? An inspiring identity, however, is memorable, especially when it is integral to our own identity. To be effective here, it's necessary for leaders to go beyond task thinking and transform the way people think about the organization. When our organization's inspiring identity exists in our minds, it satisfies the sense of purpose, significance, and pride of association we all crave. It bears repeating that unless you inspire people, you have not added this element to the work environment. And absent inspiration, people just show up for duty.

The best way to identify the various aspects of your company's inspiring identity is to bring your most innovative, passionate people together and let the ideas flow. Ask them why they are enthusiastic about their jobs. Hear their stories and those stories that inspired them. It helps to bring in creative professionals to assist you. In your sessions, answer these questions: Who are we? What do we stand for? How are we different? Where are we going? How are we going to get there? Why is it important? How do people fit in? Through this process you are likely to find the elements of your inspiring identity to build on.

Apple's Think Different ads helped to answer some of these questions and appealed primarily on an emotional level. (Steve Jobs was so moved by the ads that one magazine reporter noticed tears streaming down his face as he watched them.) FDR showed the aircraft workers the meaning of their work through a true story that resonated deeply on both rational and emotional levels. For the greatest impact on employees, leaders should answer all of the questions.

Furthermore, to reach the hearts and minds of employees, each of whom have a unique blend of learning and thinking styles, leaders should communicate the organization's story on both rational and emotional levels, employing multiple mediums such as e-mails, memorandums, presentations, voice mails, speeches, training sessions, intranet sites, and employee policies. Everything about an organization—including brands, advertisements, visual design elements, corporate voice, and hiring practices—should be consistent with the inspiring identity and therefore work together to produce an identity that moves us, just as musicians and instruments work in harmony to produce the music we love.

ELEMENT 3: KNOWLEDGE FLOW

To gain perspective on the third element of an engaging environment, we must come to understand the root cause of arguably one of the greatest incidents of managerial failure in history. It was committed by England's King George III in the 1770s when his mismanagement resulted in England's loss of the American colonies.[10] What did he do (or not do) that served to motivate a woefully underfunded and undertrained, ragtag collection of colonial citizen-soldiers to defeat the most powerful military in the world?

A combination of British condescension and presumptuous behavior toward the colonists ignited their wrath. At the time of the American Revolution, many Englishmen looked down on the colonists. With that prevailing view, it is not surprising that the king felt he could throw his considerable weight around. To raise money to pay England's debts incurred for the French and Indian War fought to protect the colonies, King George levied taxes on the colonists without their consent or the consent of their representatives. When they protested (remember the Boston Tea Party?), he answered by closing the Boston harbor, thereby cutting off the flow of goods.

Having been devalued and looked down upon, the colonists could not tolerate this dismissive act. They viewed taxation without representation as a violation of their rights as citizens of the British Empire and equated it to being treated like slaves by the English king and Parliament. The result of the king's actions was to provoke the fury of a people who already felt scorned. Thanks to King George, the 13 separate colonies came together, formed a militia, and, with reinforcements from the French and loans from the Dutch, won their independence. The government they created guaranteed a voice for *all* of its citizens (white males at that time) by protecting everyone's freedom of speech, protest, and worship.

History contains the stories of many leaders whose arrogance and failure to give people a voice in decisions that affected them contributed to their downfall: Julius Caesar, Napoleon Bonaparte, and Montezuma, to name a few. This lesson from the past seems not to have been lost on a business leader who is a serious student of history, A. G. Lafley, the CEO of Procter & Gamble (P&G).[11]

When Durk Jager resigned as CEO of P&G in June 2000, his tenure had lasted only 17 months, the shortest in the firm's 165-year history. At that time, P&G's stock had declined 50 percent, it had lost $320 million in the most recent quarter, half of its brands were losing market share, and the firm was struggling with morale problems. P&G is known for its talented brand managers and a quarter of them had left the firm.

A.G. Lafley, a low-profile, thoughtful P&G veteran, was tapped to replace Jager. From the beginning, Lafley's leadership style was a marked contrast to Jager's. Although Jager had questioned the competence of many P&G employees, Lafley immediately assured them that he knew they were capable of restoring the marketing powerhouse to its former greatness. Whereas Jager has been described as gruff and confrontational, Lafley is relentlessly inquisitive in a calm, respectful manner that builds trust with employees. Some people might judge Lafley's unassuming personality as lacking the determined will of a great leader, but they would be mistaken. Beneath Lafley's quietly confident manner resides an individual who has repeatedly demonstrated a steadfast determination to lead P&G back to greatness. To restore P&G's financial health, he cut $2 billion in costs and eliminated 9,600 jobs.

The most striking aspect of Lafley's approach has been his actions to improve the flow of knowledge throughout P&G. Lafley emphasized listening more than lecturing. During his early days as CEO, Lafley insisted on transparency by encouraging everyone to "get the mooses out of the closets." When meeting with groups of managers, he would tell them he didn't prepare a speech and just wanted to hear about the issues on their minds. A marketer to the core, Lafley also requested a study of P&G employees to hear their ideas about what needed to be done. In his desire to learn from others, he even attended meetings of P&G alumni to hear their views.

At P&G's corporate headquarters, Lafley transformed the 11th floor where senior executives maintained plush offices. Art was donated to a museum, oak walls were torn down, and 11 of the executives were moved to be closer to the people they lead. The remaining executives, including Lafley, now occupy a third of the floor in an open space with cubicles. The rest of the space was converted into a corporate training center. At the center senior executives are expected to teach many of the courses, not only for the benefit of trainees, but also to expose executives to ideas from around the world. Lafley's order to tear down "the walls" on P&G's executive floor was pragmatic and it was loaded with symbolism. These actions signaled his intention to tear down the walls that prevented knowledge, the lifeblood of every organization, from flowing throughout P&G.

It wasn't long after Lafley became CEO that employee morale improved and P&G's performance improved along with it. After the first year of Lafley's tenure as CEO, the number of employees who strongly agreed with the statement "We're on the right track to deliver business results" soared from 18 percent to 49 percent. And in a little more than two years after taking over, Lafley restored P&G to profitability and increased its stock price by 70 percent. To the amazement of Wall Street, Lafley orchestrated P&G's turnaround during a recessionary economic environment.

In stark contrast to the approach of King George III, A.G. Lafley informed and sought the views of those he led. This aspect of an engaging environment we describe as *knowledge flow* and define it as follows:

When everyone in the organization participates in an open, honest, and safe dialogue where leaders seek and consider diverse viewpoints in order to understand people, identify the best ideas, and make superior decisions.

When a high degree of knowledge flow exists, everyone feels like a part of the team. It also brings about organizational unity and alignment by helping people to become "of one mind."

In addition to motivating and uniting employees, knowledge flow also directly benefits leaders. It helps them make better decisions by arming them with knowledge from people on the front lines closest to their customers and competitors. Organizations whose leaders make better decisions are more successful. And winning motivates everyone, especially those people who work directly with a company's customers.

Here are a few ways to stimulate knowledge flow in any organization.

1. *Embrace the belief that no one has a monopoly on ideas and actively seek ideas and input.* To improve knowledge flow, it is necessary for everyone to believe they must share their viewpoints. This includes views about what's right, what's wrong, and what's missing from leaders' thinking. In asking for opinions, leaders should be prepared to deal with employees whose manner and tone can only be described as irritating. When people become emotional, leaders need to maintain their composure and listen closely to the message. Just remember, the irritation that occurs when a grain of sand enters an oyster is necessary to produce one of nature's most beautiful creations—the pearl.

2. *Regularly conduct knowledge flow sessions.* Leaders throughout an organization should frequently hold what we call knowledge flow sessions. These are meetings with groups of employees to keep them apprised of business developments and to hear their thoughts. Key to the success of these sessions is for leaders to share their thinking on important issues and create an environment where people feel safe sharing their views, especially when those views are at odds with the views held by their leaders or peers. This is different from the typical town hall meeting where little discussion takes place. People often withhold potentially valuable viewpoints because they are afraid to speak the truth to those in power, and so it is important to foster a tolerant atmosphere where diverse opinions are brought out into the open for consideration.

3. *Make information widely available, especially on important decisions that require widespread execution, and when sufficient time exists to allow for broad dialogue.* High-quality dialogue in knowledge flow sessions requires well-informed participants. This, in turn, requires the broad dissemination of knowledge. Management information should be posted on a secure intranet site for easy

access as well as explained in face-to-face meetings. Most companies fear that information will end up in their competitors' hands. Our advice is to err in favor of greater transparency by making information as widely available as possible. Even if it does end up in a competitor's hands, in most cases the benefit that comes from informing people within the organization will far outweigh the benefit to your competitor.

To sum it up, King George III impeded knowledge flow by refusing to give the colonists a voice and his actions alienated them. A. G. Lafley increased knowledge flow by giving P&G employees a voice, and he saw P&G's performance and employee morale improve.

Before we go on, let's summarize what we've covered so far. When leaders demonstrate that they *value* people, when they impart an inspiring identity that provides people a *vision* of who they are and where they are going, and when leaders give people a *voice* by encouraging knowledge flow, something magical happens: people become engaged. *Value + Vision + Voice = Victory for the Organization* is an easy way to remember what we refer to as the *core elements* of an engaging work environment.

To give everyone value, vision, and voice, it is necessary to have two very special types of people in the organization. These two different types of people enable the organization to realize an engaging environment by making the core elements happen. What we refer to as *enabling elements*, the final two elements of an engaging environment, are committed members and servant leaders.

ELEMENT 4: COMMITTED MEMBERS

The next element of an engaging environment is seen in the life of a Frenchman honored at several historical sites in the state of Virginia.[12] What will surprise you if you visit these sites are the recurring tributes to this man whose name and story remain unknown to most Americans today. At Monticello, Thomas Jefferson's hilltop home near Charlottesville, you'll find a portrait and bust of the Frenchman. At Mount Vernon, Washington's home on the Potomac River, you'll learn that Washington thought of him like a son and you will find the key to the Bastille on display, sent by the Frenchman to Washington after he ordered the notorious Paris prison torn down during the French Revolution. Perhaps most surprising of all, in the Hall of Presidents in the Rotunda of the Virginia capitol where a statue of George Washington and busts of the other seven Virginia-born U.S. presidents reside, you'll find a sculptured bust of the Frenchman who was neither a president nor born in the state.

Across the United States, more than 600 villages, towns, cities, counties, lakes, educational institutions, and other landmarks are named after him. Every year on the fourth of July, the American Ambassador to France and the senior-most American military advisor in the country travel to his gravesite to replace the American flag that flies over it. The gravesite is unusual in France, for the Frenchman's casket and that of his wife lie beneath soil taken from Bunker Hill, the site outside of Boston, Massachusetts, where one of the first battles in the Revolutionary War occurred.

As you might guess, this Frenchman was far from ordinary. His name is Marie-Joseph-Paul-Yves-Gilbert du Motier de La Fayette, more commonly known as The Marquis de Lafayette.

Lafayette was one of the wealthiest young men in France. Despite his position, his early life had not been easy. Lafayette's father, a colonel of grenadiers, was killed in battle when Lafayette was 2 years old, and his mother and grandfather died when he was 12. By age 14 he had joined the Royal Army and at age 16 he married Marie Adrienne Francoise de Noailles, a wealthy relative of the King of France.

In his late teens Lafayette became enamored with the cause of American independence. At a dinner he attended, Lafayette heard the Duke of Gloucester, a brother of England's King George III, share his strong opposition to the English treatment of American colonists. It seems from that point on, Lafayette began to develop a consuming desire to see the American colonists achieve their independence.

At age 19, Lafayette purchased a ship, named it the *Victoire*, and persuaded several French army officers to join him in helping the Americans. After he arrived in America, Lafayette approached John Hancock, head of the Continental Congress, and volunteered his services. In a letter to Hancock, Lafayette, like the signers of the Declaration of Independence, pledged his "life, his fortune and his sacred honor" to American independence. Lafayette was inspired by America's cause, and his inspiration led him to make a commitment to do everything he possibly could to achieve it.

Lafayette was commissioned as a major general and eventually became an aide-de-camp to the Continental Army's Commander-in-Chief George Washington. Historian Arthur M. Schlesinger Jr. noted that Lafayette "distinguished himself militarily . . . was an essential actor in the successful plan to trap the British Army under General Cornwallis at Yorktown . . . [and became] an invaluable ally of American minister to France, Thomas Jefferson"

Perhaps most important, when Lafayette went back to France to secure resources for the Americans, he returned with an army of 4,000 soldiers and a fleet of ships commanded by Count de Rochambeau. Before Lafayette's return, the American effort was losing steam after suffering several defeats. Lafayette's return, his infectious optimism, and the resources he brought combined to revitalize the American effort.

Lafayette promoted the elements of an engaging environment. He consistently promoted the core element of human value. He spent a considerable amount of his personal wealth to purchase shoes and clothes for the men in his command. Although he could afford to buy a house to stay warm, he chose to remain with the common soldiers at Valley Forge during the freezing winter of 1778. He fought alongside the infantrymen, even dismounting his horse if necessary to be closer to them. Lafayette treated common soldiers with respect. He was motivated by the core element of inspiring identity. Later in life he would comment: "To have participated in the toils and perils of the unspotted struggle for independence . . . the foundation of the American era of a new social order . . . has been the pride, the encouragement, the support of [my] long and eventful life." He embraced the core element of knowledge flow by seeking the opinions of his soldiers, asking them what worked and what didn't work in the battles they had fought. Lafayette later claimed that the common soldiers were his greatest teachers. The soldiers were so fond of Lafayette they referred to him as "Our Marquis."

Lafayette elevated the mission of America over self-interest. The author Harlow Giles Unger described it well when he said: "[Lafayette] fled from incomparable luxury . . . to wade through the South Carolina swamps, freeze at Valley Forge, and ride through the stifling summer heat of Virginia—as an unpaid volunteer, fighting and bleeding for liberty, in a land not his own, for a people not his own."

More recently another individual demonstrated a remarkable commitment to a cause and to his teammates. This individual was not to be found on the battlefield, however, but instead in the arenas around America where people gathered to witness a basketball legend in the making.

When Michael Jordan began playing in the NBA for the Chicago Bulls, he epitomized excellence as an individual contributor.[13] His superhuman feats over the course of five seasons, however, were not enough to make champions out of the Bulls. Not until Phil Jackson became head coach and began to influence the young superstar did the Bulls finally make it to the big game.

Jackson helped Jordan see the need to go beyond being a star, to become, in Jackson's words, a player "who surrenders the me for the we." In the context of the Bulls this meant playing within the triangle offense that Jackson taught. Jordan, commenting on Jackson's team orientation, remarked that he "enhanced. . . . [our] ability to be better teammates . . . without taking away [our] individuality."

Until that time Jordan thought he needed to win games on his own because he didn't have confidence that his teammates would perform in the clutch. A one-man show, however, even if it was a show put on by one of the game's greatest players, was never going to be enough to get the Bulls to the top.

So Jordan adjusted. His contribution to the Bulls's success rose to a new level. He began spending more time with his teammates on and off the court. Writing about the experience in his book *Sacred Hoops*, Phil Jackson observed:

"Jordan's presence [affected] the psyche of the team . . . he challenged everyone to step up . . . before practice I often found him working one-on-one with young players."

Beginning in 1991, when the Bulls won their first world championship, the contributions of Jordan's teammates increased dramatically. In the past, when the score was close at the end of a game, Jordan always wanted the ball. After Jackson worked with Jordan, he trusted his teammates to make the big play during several pivotal situations.

One such instance came during game six of the 1993 championship against the Phoenix Suns. Near the end of the game and down by a score of 98 to 96, the Bulls came down court and instead of passing the ball to Jordan, the Bulls got the ball to John Paxson who shot and scored a three-point jumper just before the buzzer went off to win the game. The press hailed it as the shot heard around the world. The next year in the final championship game against the Utah Jazz, Jordan passed the ball to his teammate Steve Kerr who hit a jump shot just before the buzzer to clinch another championship for the Bulls. Over the course of eight years, the Chicago Bulls won an astounding six world championship titles.

Before he left the Los Angeles Lakers in 2004, Phil Jackson achieved a career record of 832 wins and 316 losses (a .725 winning percentage), making him the coach with the best winning percentage in NBA history. Along the way Jackson won nine NBA championships between coaching the Chicago Bulls and the Los Angeles Lakers.

One of the primary reasons for his success was that he encouraged his players to commit to becoming team players. Michael Jordan responded to Jackson's encouragement by humbly making a personal commitment to his team and teammates rather than pridefully continuing on as a one-man show to the detriment of his team's performance. Marquis de Lafayette and Michael Jordan were *committed members*. We define this element as follows:

People who are committed to the mission, their fellow members, and to teamwork while playing their specific role within the whole of the organization. Committed members embrace human value, share the inspiring identity, and engage in knowledge flow.

Leaders cultivate committed members by highlighting the values of a committed member as being part of the team's identity and asking everyone to make a commitment to them. The first and foremost commitment must come from leaders. In fact, no one should ever be allowed to lead others unless he or she has first proved to be a committed member. Out of the ranks of committed members arise the second type of people who are necessary to create an engaging environment: servant leaders.

ELEMENT 5: SERVANT LEADERS

The final element of an engaging environment is embodied in the life of one of the greatest leaders of all time. When you read the accounts of those remarkable individuals who contributed to the founding of America—John and Abigail Adams, Benjamin Franklin, Alexander Hamilton, Thomas Jefferson, and James Madison—it is especially striking to see how they viewed George Washington as being, unquestionably, the greatest leader among them.[14] What was it about this quiet, dignified Virginian that made him so extraordinary to those who knew him?

Richard Neustadt, Presidential Scholar at Harvard University, observed the following about George Washington: "It wasn't his generalship that made him stand out. . . . It was the way he attended to and stuck by his men. His soldiers knew that he respected and cared for them, and that he would share their severe hardships."

From the time he was a young man, George Washington kept a personal rule book to remind him of the behavior that he aspired to live out each day. Many of the rules capture the respect and deference Washington showed for others throughout his life. Here are some of the entries: "Every action done in company ought to be done with some sign of respect to those who are present," "Speak not when you should hold your peace;" "Use no reproachful language against anyone;" "Submit your judgment to others with modesty;" "When another speaks be attentive;" "Think before you speak;" and "be not so desirous to overcome as not to give liberty to each one to deliver his opinion."

Like many other great leaders who engage their followers, George Washington placed the mission and the needs of those around him above his own interests.

- The historian Edward G. Lengel described Washington's leadership during the extraordinarily cold winter of 1777–1778 at Valley Forge as "sacrificial" and noted that "he took great care in seeing that his soldiers were well-housed."

- Washington's sacrifice for America was supported by the facts that he served as commander of the Continental Army without pay and, as Historian Henry Steele Commager noted, was nearly bankrupt by the time he returned home to Mount Vernon after serving as president.

- Historian Barbara Tuchman, called Washington "a true hero . . . a remarkable man in every aspect of his character, in his courage, in his persistence . . . in spite of enormous frustration and difficulties [he faced]."

- On one occasion when approached by soldiers who wanted to overthrow the government because they had not been paid, Washington made it clear that the idea repulsed him, under no circumstances would he ever consider it, and it should never be mentioned again.

- When he resigned his military commission without seizing political power, King George III, commented that, if it were true, Washington was truly the greatest man in the world.

Nearly two centuries after Washington's death another servant leader emerged in Stamford, Connecticut, not far from many of the battlefields where Washington fought against the British. Like Washington, this leader would lead her people through a time when the odds were against them and survival was questionable. Here's her story.

Anne Mulcahy, the CEO of Xerox, is an optimistic realist.[15] After becoming CEO and bringing herself up to speed on Xerox's situation, she shocked Wall Street by announcing that Xerox's business model was unsustainable, a remark that caused Xerox stock to drop 26 percent the next day.

Despite her realization that Xerox faced serious challenges, she knew from her 27 years at the firm that it could be revived. "A lot of people will try to convince you that there are advantages to Chapter 11 . . . [but I said], 'Don't even go there.' Whatever you think they are from a financial standpoint, I think they are dismal and demoralizing for a company that wants desperately to turn around and regain its reputation." She was determined to lead Xerox back to health stating "sometimes you can will your way through things ... as much as you need competence, luck and hard work, I think will has a lot to do with it."

In addition to her optimism, another thing that stands out about Anne Mulcahy is how she elevates human value. "Nothing spooked me as much as waking up in the middle of the night and thinking about 96,000 people and retirees and what would happen if this thing went south," stated Mulcahy in a 2003 interview with *Fortune*. And when, to keep Xerox afloat, she had to shut down a business she had previously built up and lay off many of the people she had hired, Mulcahy went to meet them face-to-face. "The company was in a lot of trouble. They weren't the ones accountable for the problem," she said. So she did the only thing she could: "take the hit personally ... I hung out, walked the halls, and told them I was sorry." Mulcahy made the tough decision and carried it out in a way that preserved the dignity of the people involved.

Her empathy and presence among them are a stark contrast to some leaders who by their physical and/or emotional absence abandon employees in their time of need. One company we know had the employees in a division attend an off-site meeting where it was announced the division would be shut down that very day. Security guards were present and employees were required to immediately collect their personal effects from their offices. At the meeting members of senior management were conspicuously absent. It's no surprise that the workers were outraged at how they were treated after their years of dedicated service to the company.

Anne Mulcahy also promotes the elements of inspiring identity and knowledge flow. She boosted employee morale by logging 100,000 miles to visit Xerox employees in her first year. She listened to them, too. "People around you want to please . . . that's where honest critics can play an important role. Encourage them to tell it like it is," she said. According to her colleagues, she "told us everything, stuff we didn't want to know [like how close they were to running out of cash]." "Part of her DNA is to tell you the good, the bad, and the ugly," remarked one colleague.

She asked Xerox employees to be committed to the turnaround: "save every dollar as if it were your own." And she rewarded those committed members who stayed at Xerox by refusing to eliminate raises and extending small perks like time off from work on their birthdays.

One observer noted: "She was leading by example. Everyone at Xerox knew she was working hard, and that she was working hard for them." *Fortune* noted that she hadn't had a weekend off in two years, frequently visited three cities a day, carried her own luggage on flights, and did more cooking on the Xerox corporate jet than she had at her own home. She was clearly sacrificing for the sake of the mission and for the Xerox family.

Anne Mulcahy's infectious optimism and hard work paid off. When Mulcahy was named Xerox's CEO in May 2000, the firm was on the verge of bankruptcy and its stock had dropped from $63.69 a share to $4.43. After she took charge, Xerox employees rallied to support her. Together they restored Xerox to profitability and positioned the firm for future growth, prompting Nick Nicholas, a Xerox board member and former CEO of Time Warner, to proclaim "the story here is a minor miracle."

Anne Mulcahy strived to be a leader to whom people could be devoted, a leader who they knew would give it her all to save the company they were counting on. To those of us observing Xerox from the outside it seemed that Xerox was Anne Mulcahy's ailing child and she would do everything in her power get it back on its feet, or die trying. The same could be said about George Washington whom Americans have always referred to as the father of their country.

George Washington and Anne Mulcahy are examples of *servant leaders*. We define this element as follows:

Committed members entrusted with the authority to direct the efforts of others in order to accomplish the mission and help fellow members achieve their potential. Servant leaders establish and maintain the processes necessary to create an engaging environment and they serve as role models to others.[16]

Servant leaders are selfless not selfish, they show humility not arrogance, they are magnanimous not vengeful, and they are guided by the courage of their convictions rather than the need to be popular. Servant leaders assume a leadership role not to feed their egos, but for the sake of doing something they believe is important.

The selfless behavior of Washington and other servant leaders engages people because it promotes trust. When a leader demonstrates that he or she is leading for the sake of the mission and the people, rather than for self-serving purposes, people naturally become more trusting and devoted to the leader.

Of course, no leader or environment is perfect. George Washington had slaves until they were set free after his wife Martha's death. FDR failed in the area of human value on several occasions, including when he approved the internment of Japanese-Americans during World War II and when he failed to get behind the passage of federal antilynching legislation. Despite the imperfections in the environments maintained by these leaders, they strived to improve the environments they were responsible for, and for the most part they succeeded.

Every leader should take note of George Washington and Anne Mulcahy's example. Leaders throughout your organization must become servant leaders to bring out the best efforts of employees in their individual roles within the organization and to maximize trust and cooperation among them. By putting the right leadership training, metrics, and accountability in place, it can be done. Without these essential components and a process in place to implement them, an organization will not develop servant leaders or sustain peak performance. Transformation is not accidental. It comes about only when leaders are intentional in their efforts to make it happen. The legendary UCLA basketball coach John Wooden said it best, "failing to prepare is preparing to fail."

CONCLUSION

In this chapter, we've introduced the five elements that produce an engaging environment and examples of leaders who employed at least some of them. A more comprehensive explanation of the processes and best practices is beyond the scope of this chapter; however, we hope our ideas have provided a vision of what is possible.

Research has proven that organizations with higher employee engagement experience *higher* customer satisfaction, profits, productivity, and *lower* employee turnover and accidents.[17] An engaging environment not only makes work more personally satisfying, but it has a definite impact on the bottom line.

We've given you the elements that create an engaging work environment, one that will generate the positive energy and enthusiasm that attracts employees (and customers) like a magnet. The great leaders we wrote about realized tremendous success implementing some of these elements. Just imagine what your company would be like if all five elements were present in your work environment. Your company will come alive with greater trust, cooperation, optimism, innovation, and productivity. Now that's the kind of place where we all want to work and where customers will want to come back to time and time again.

NOTES

This chapter is adapted from material in the authors' forthcoming book on what engages and energizes people on the front lines in service businesses.

The authors would like to thank Katharine Stallard and Mitchell Dickey for their contributions to this chapter.

1. J. Rufus Fears, *A History of Freedom,* lectures by Professor J. Rufus Fears, Professor of Classics at the University of Oklahoma (The Teaching Company, 2001), CD-ROM.

2. Gordon S. Wood, *The Radicalism of the American Revolution* (New York: Alfred A. Knopf, 1992): 6–7.

3. James McGregor Burns, *Leadership,* (New York: Harper & Row, 1979): 10, 27–28; James R. Gaines, *Evening in the Palace of Reason: Bach Meets Frederick the Great in the Age of Enlightenment* (New York: Fourth Estate, 2005): 194–212, 245–248.

4. Ani Hadjian, "Follow the Leader," *Fortune* (November 27, 1995): 96; Sally Helgesen, *The Female Advantage: Women's Ways of Leadership* (New York: Doubleday, 1995): 71–103; John A. Byrne, "Profiting From the Nonprofits," *Business Week* (March 26, 1990): 66–74; Frances Hesselbein, "The Power of Civility," *Leader to Leader,* No. 5 Summer 1997, http://www.leadertoleader.org/leaderbooks/l2l/summer97/fh.htl.

5. Barbara S. Peterson, *Blue Streak: Inside JetBlue, the Upstart That Rocked an Industry,* (New York: Portfolio, 2004): xiv; Howard Schultz and Dori Jones Yang, *Pour Your Heart Into It: How Starbucks Built a Company One Cup at a Time* (New York: Hyperion, 1997): 245.

6. Doris Kearns Goodwin, *No Ordinary Time: Franklin and Eleanor Roosevelt: The Home Front in World War II* (New York: Simon & Schuster, 1994): 340.

7. *Encarta Encyclopedia Online,* s.v. "Aircraft Production During World War II," http://encarta.msn.com/media_701500594_761563737_-1_1/Aircraft_Production_During_World_War_II.html (accessed June 1, 2005).

8. Alan Deutschman, *The Second Coming of Steve Jobs* (New York: Broadway Books, 2000), 251–253; Stuart Elliott, "Apple Endorses Some Achievers Who "Think Different," *The New York Times,* August 3, 1998.

9. Laurence D. Ackerman, *Identity Is Destiny: Leadership and the Roots of Value Creation* (San Francisco: Berrett-Kohler, 2000): x.

10. Bernard Bailyn, *Ideological Origins of the American Revolution* (Cambridge: Harvard University Press, 1967): 232–233; Barbara W. Tuchman, *The March of Folly: From Troy to Vietnam* (New York: Alfred A. Knopf, 1984): 128–231.

11. Beth Belton, "Procter & Gamble's Renovator-in-Chief," *Business Week Online,* December 11, 2002, http://www.businessweek.com/bwdaily/dnflash/dec2002/nf20021211_7599.htm; Robert Berner, "A Catalyst and Encourager of

Change," *Business Week Online*, July 7, 2003, http://www.businessweek.com/print/magazine/content/03_27/b3840014_mz001.htm; Katrina Booker, "The Un-CEO," *Fortune*, September 16, 2002, 88–96; Cliff Peale, "The Lafley Method," *The Cincinnati Enquirer Online*, June 9, 2002, http://www.enquirer.com/editions/2002/06/09/fin_the_lafley_method.html; James R. Stengel, Andrea L. Dixon, and Chris T. Allen, "Listening Begins at Home," *Harvard Business Review* (November 2003): 106–116.

12. Harlow Giles Unger, *Lafayette* (Hoboken: John Wiley & Sons, 2002): xiii–xxiii, 4–16, 26–30, 58–71, 108–117; Marian Klamkin, *The Return of Lafayette* (New York: Charles Scribner's Sons, 1975): 1–7, 193; Arthur M. Schlesinger Jr. and John S. Bowman, eds., *The Almanac of American History* (New York: G. P. Putnam's Sons, 1983): 126.

13. Phil Jackson and Hugh Delehanty, *Sacred Hoops: Spiritual Lessons of a Hardwood Warrior* (New York: Hyperion, 1995): 15–22.

14. Joseph J. Ellis, *His Excellency: George Washington* (New York: Alfred A. Knopf, 2004): xiv; Philip Kunhardt Jr., Philip Kunhardt III, and Peter W. Kunhardt, "The Heroic Posture," *The American President*, videocassette, (Alexandria, Va.: PBS Home Video, Burbank, Calif.: Warner Home Video, 2000); Bill Moyers edited by Betty Sue Flowers, *A World of Ideas* (New York: Doubleday, 1989): 8–9, 229; Edward Lengel, e-mail message to author, April 8, 2005.

15. Betsy Morris, "The Accidental CEO," *Fortune Online*, June 9, 2003, http://www.fortune.com/fortune/print/0,15935,457272,00.html; Olga Kharif, "Anne Mulcahy Has Xerox by the Horns," *Business Week Online*, May 29, 2003, http://www.businessweek.com/technology/content/may2003/tc20030529_1642_tc111.htm.

16. The term *Servant Leader* was first coined by Robert K. Greenleaf in an article entitled "Servant to Leader," published in 1970.

17. James K. Hart, Frank L. Schmidt, and Theodore L. Hayes, "Business-Unit-Level Relationship Between Employee Satisfaction, Employee Engagement, and Business Outcomes: A Meta-Analysis," *Journal of Applied Psychology* 87(2) (2002):268–279.

Index

About the Editor and Contributors

EDITOR

REGINA FAZIO MARUCA is a freelance business writer and editor, specializing in marketing/branding and leadership. Formerly a Senior Editor at the *Harvard Business Review* (*HBR*), she has conducted interviews with dozens of high-profile business leaders and thinkers for *HBR* and, later on, for *Fast Company*. Before working at *HBR*, she was a reporter and editor at *Boston Business Journal* and at *New England Business Magazine*. Since leaving *HBR* in 2000, she has provided editorial, writing, and research services for authors at such organizations as Harvard Business School, Bain & Co., Accenture, The Center for Executive Development, Boston University, and the Committee of 200 (for women entrepreneurs and business leaders) and is currently co-authoring, with Rob Galford, *Your Leadership Legacy* (Harvard Business School Press, 2006).

CONTRIBUTORS

GARY ADAMSON has devoted his career to expanding the boundaries of what's possible. He began his career as Vice President of Swedish Health Systems in Denver, Colorado, where he started the nation's first and most comprehensive hospital-based wellness program, and consulted with hundreds of hospitals on how to build healthier communities. Five years later, he founded a healthcare advertising and consulting company, where he spent the next 16 years working in every part of the United States with health systems, hospitals, foundations, medical groups, health plans, healthcare associations, and a wide variety of businesses to develop unified innovations in strategy, operations, and communications. In addition to being a highly rated speaker at regional, national, and international conferences, Gary is owner and Chief Experience Officer of Starizon, Inc., an Experience Design firm, helping clients design the experiences that would significantly transform them and strengthen their brand success.

MARIE BELL is a research associate at the Harvard Business School. She has worked with faculty writing numerous case studies and teaching notes as well as in industry in the hospitality sector in marketing and finance roles. Bell received an MBA from Harvard Business School in 1989 and a BA from Simon Fraser University in 1982.

JENNY DAVIS-PECCOUD is the manager of Bain & Company's global organization practice, based in London. She has worked with companies in a number of industries, including consumer products, retail, manufacturing, and utilities. Her organizational experience includes comprehensive organization redesign, decision accountabilities, process enhancement, overhead optimization, and organization integration.

CAROLYN DEWING-HOMMES is a co-founder and partner at Greenwich, Connecticut-based E Pluribus Partners, a consulting firm that specializes in leadership development and coaching to unlock the potential of individuals and organizations. Previously she spent 15 years at Citibank working in New York City, Sao Paulo, London, and Hong Kong. At Citibank she was selected to lead a global team, reporting to the CEO, which identified the best practices of companies worldwide that successfully engaged their employees, specifically in the area of work/life balance. Carolyn's industry experience comes out of corporate and private banking where she managed significant client relationships in Europe, Asia, and Latin America.

WOODRUFF W. DRIGGS is the managing Director of the Accenture Customer Relationship Management (CRM) Global Service Line. Based in Boston, Woody directs the worldwide growth and market leadership of the CRM business for the company.

ROBERT M. GALFORD is a managing partner of the Center for Executive Development. He divides his time between teaching in Executive Education programs and working closely with senior executives on the issues that lie at the intersection of strategy and organization. He is the co-author of *The Trusted Advisor* (with David Maister and Charles Green, *The Trusted Leader* (with Anne Drapeau), and *The Leadership Legacy* (with Regina Maruca, 2006).

JODY HOFFER GITTELL is Assistant Professor of management at the Heller Graduate School, Brandeis University, where she specializes in the theory of relational coordination: coordinating work through relationships of shared goals, shared knowledge, and mutual respect. Her research explores how front-line employees contribute to quality and efficiency outcomes in service settings, with a particular focus on the airline and healthcare industries. She has published in such journals as the *Harvard Business Review, Organization Science,* the *International Journal of Human Resource Management,* and *California Management Review* and has contributed to several books including *Positive Organizational Scholarship* (edited by Kim Cameron, et al., 2003) and *Consumer Driven Health Care* (edited by Regina Herzlinger, 2003). She is the author of *The Southwest Airlines Way: Using the Power of Relationships to Achieve High Performance* (2003).

MONICA HIGGINS is Associate Professor in the Organizational Behavior Unit at the Harvard Business School, where she teaches Self-Assessment and Career Development in the MBA program and Strategic Human Resources Management in the executive education program. Before joining the faculty at Harvard, she worked in Personal Card Acquisition for American Express Travel Related Services and in the Capital Markets Technologies Division for BankBoston. Professor Higgins also spent approximately five years as a consultant for Bain & Company in their Boston office and for Harbridge House, an international organizational change consulting firm based in Boston. Her current research focuses on the relational context in which careers are shaped and organizational decisions are made including a longitudinal study of the career choices and work lives of Harvard MBA students and a study of the careers of senior executives in the biotech industry. Her recent book on this topic, *Career Imprints: Creating Leaders Across an Industry,* was published in April 2005 and is part of Warren Bennis's Leadership Development Series.

RACHEL E. HILL is a consultant with FTI Helios Consulting Group. Her specialty is internal and external communication. Before joining FTI Helios, she worked with Americorps and has served as a researcher for several books including *Radical Marketing, Monopoly Rules,* and *60 Trends in 60 Minutes.*

SAM I. HILL is a Senior Managing Director with FTI Helios and spends most of his time helping Chief Marketing Officers and Chief Executive Officers develop breakthrough growth strategies. He began his career at Kraft General Foods, first working as an engineer in a plant and later serving as Director of International Strategy. Much of his career has been spent as a management consultant with Booz-Allen & Hamilton, where he was lead partner serving clients and leading the Global Marketing Innovation Task Force. Immediately before forming Helios, he was Vice Chairman and Chief Strategic Officer of D'Arcy Masius Benton & Bowles, the twelfth largest ad agency in the world. Sam is recognized as a leading thinker on the topics of growth, marketing and branding. His work has appeared in such publications as the *Harvard Business Review, Strategy & Business, Sloan Management Review, Brandweek, Journal of Business Strategy, Ad Age, Fortune,* and the *Financial Times.* His books include *Radical Marketing* (co-authored with Glenn Rifkin, 2000), *The Infinite Asset* (co-authored with Chris Lederer, 2001), and *Sixty Trends in Sixty Minutes* (2002).

JODI KROUPA has spent her entire career immersed in all aspects of communications. First, she served as an account executive for two different advertising/consulting agencies in Denver, Colorado and Seattle, Washington. At the agencies, she provided various healthcare, high-tech, and commercial real estate clients with communications and strategy consultation—helping them to effectively build memorable, differentiated brands within their particular industry, on local, regional, and national levels. Being an Inspirational Immersion Guide at Starizon, Inc. has allowed her to reignite her passion for writing and has provided unlimited opportunities for capitalizing on her marketing and advertising expertise. Her proudest accomplishment to date was authoring the story and managing all production aspects of "The Riddle of the Sphinx" corporate storytelling engagement for San Juan Regional Medical Center.

EDWARD E. LAWLER III is Distinguished Professor at the University of Southern California Marshall School of Business and founder and director of the university's Center for Effective Organization. He is the author of many influential article and books on human resource management and organizational behavior including *Treat People Right!* (2003) and *Built to Change* (2006).

JAY W. LORSCH is the Louis Kirstein Professor of Human Relations at the Harvard Business School. He is the author of more than a dozen books, the most recent of which are *Back to the Drawing Board: Designing Boards for a Complex World* (with Colin B. Carter, 2003), *Aligning the Stars: How to Succeed When Professionals Drive Results* (with Thomas J. Tierney, 2002), and *Pawns or Potentates: The Reality of America's Corporate Boards* (1989). *Organization and Environment* (with Paul R. Lawrence) won the Academy of Management's Best Management Book of the Year Award and the James A. Hamilton Book Award of the College of Hospital Administrators in 1969.

PAUL F. NUNES is a Partner and an Executive Research Fellow at the Accenture Institute for High Performance Business in Wellesley, Massachusetts. He is the co-author, with Brian Johnson, of *Mass Affluence: 7 New Rules of Marketing to Today's Consumer* (2004).

JASON PANKAU is a co-founder and Partner at Greenwich, Connecticut-based E Pluribus Partners, a consulting firm that specializes in leadership development and coaching to unlock the potential of individuals and organizations. He also serves as an associate pastor at Stanwich Congregational Church in Greenwich, Connecticut, where he focuses on mentoring and leadership development. He serves as a consultant and life coach to many corporate executives and ministers, advising them on both personal and professional matters. He is also a frequent speaker on leadership and mentoring leaders.

B. JOSEPH PINE II is an author, speaker, and management advisor to Fortune 500 companies and entrepreneurial start-ups alike. As an owner, senior guide, and coach with Starizon Inc., he provides extraordinary scholarship, insight, and creativity to the client experience. Joe co-wrote the best-selling business book *The Experience Economy: Work Is Theatre & Every Business a Stage* (1999), which describes the emerging consumer quest for experiences—memorable events that engage customers in an inherently personal way. In addition, Joe has written numerous articles for the *Harvard Business Review, The Wall Street Journal, Chief Executive, Worldlink, CIO,* and *Health Forum,* among others, along with the award-winning business book *Mass Customization: The New Frontier in Business Competition.* In his speaking and teaching engagements, Joe has addressed the World Economic Forum and is a Visiting Professor at the University of Amsterdam, a recurring guest lecturer at MIT Sloan School of Management, and a Senior Fellow with both the Design Futures Council and the European Centre for the Experience Economy, which he co-founded.

TON PLEKKENPOL owns the Quasar Group, a consulting firm that specializes in revitalizing management teams and employees and jump-starting their creativity. He is also chairman of the Renaissance Group, a part of the Dutch Social and Economic Council, and he is an affiliate of the European Center of the Experience Economy, which partners with Joe Pine.

V. KASTURI (KASH) RANGAN is the Malcolm P. McNair Professor of Marketing at the Harvard Business School and, until recently, the chairman of the Marketing Department (1998–2002). He has taught a wide variety of MBA courses, including the core First-Year Marketing course, and the second-year electives, Business Marketing and Channels-to-Market. He has also taught marketing in the Advanced Management Program for senior managers. Currently, Rangan teaches the elective course, Social Marketing, and a number of focused executive programs: Channels to Market, Business Marketing Strategy, Strategic Perspectives on Nonprofit Management, and Governance for Nonprofit Excellence. Professor Rangan's business marketing and channels research has appeared in management journals such as *Journal of Marketing, Harvard Business Review, Sloan Management Review, Journal of Retailing, Management Science, Marketing Science,* and *Organization Science.* Rangan has authored several books including *Going to Market* (co-authored with E. Raymond Corey and Frank V. Cespedes, 1999) and *Business Marketing Strategy* (co-authored with Benson B. Shapiro and Rowland T. Moriarty, 1995). Rangan currently serves on the editorial board of *Journal of Retailing* and *Journal of Business-to-Business Marketing.*

JEFFREY F. RAYPORT is founder and chairman of Marketspace LLC, a strategic advisory business that works with leading service-oriented companies to create sustainable competitive advantage in the networked economy. Marketspace LLC is a unit of Monitor Group, a global strategy services and merchant banking firm.

For nearly a decade, Rayport was a faculty member at Harvard Business School. He continues to focus his research on new information technologies and their impacts on companies' service and marketing strategies, particularly in information-intensive industries. As a consultant, Rayport has worked with executives and corporations around the world, specializing in the development of breakthrough service strategies for network-based businesses, particularly in consumer marketing, media, entertainment, and financial services. With co-author Bernard J. Jaworski, Rayport has published three leading MBA-level textbooks on strategy in the networked economy (*e-Commerce, Cases in e-Commerce,* and *Introduction to e-Commerce*) and a trade book on service strategies in the digital age, *Best Face Forward: Why Companies Must Improve Their Service Interfaces with Customers* (2005).

Prior to joining the HBS faculty, Rayport was a reporter for *Fortune*, a telecommunications analyst for Nikko Securities (in Tokyo), and a principal of the Winthrop Group, a consulting firm specializing in the history of business and technology. His writing has appeared in a variety of publications, including *The Boston Globe, CIO Magazine, CMO Magazine, Financial Times, Fast Company, Fortune, Harvard Business Review, Harvard Magazine, The Industry Standard, The Los Angeles Times, McKinsey Quarterly, Optimize,* and *Strategy & Business*, and he has appeared on numerous occasions as a business commentator on public television and radio, including *The Lehrer NewsHour* on PBS and *Marketplace, TechNation,* and *The Connection* on National Public Radio.

Rayport earned an AB from Harvard College, an M.Phil. in International Relations at University of Cambridge (United Kingdom), an AM in the History of American Civilization at Harvard University, and a PhD at Harvard in Business History. He serves as a director of several public and private corporations, including Andrews McMeel Universal, Exit 41, GSI Commerce (GSIC), International Data Group, and ValueClick (VCLK).

PAUL ROGERS is a director of Bain & Company, based in the London office, and the leader of Bain's global organization practice. He has worked with a wide range of retail and consumer products clients on issues including growth and competitive strategy; organizational effectiveness; customer, cost, and brand management; acquisition evaluation; postmerger integration; and the management of company-wide change. Paul's organizational experience spans comprehensive organizational redesign, leadership, decision making, culture change, talent management, front-line employee loyalty, overhead optimization, and change management. He has helped clients improve organizational effectiveness in a wide range of industries including telecommunications, financial services, healthcare, chemicals, utilities, and business services. He leads Bain's ongoing multiyear global research into "High Performance Organizations."

MICHAEL LEE STALLARD is President and a co-founder of Greenwich, Connecticut-based E Pluribus Partners, a consulting firm that specializes in leadership development and coaching to unlock the potential of individuals and organizations. Previously he was chief marketing officer for business units of Morgan Stanley and Charles Schwab. Earlier in his career Michael worked in marketing, finance, business development, and strategy roles at Morgan Stanley's Van Kampen Investments business, Barclays de Zoete Wedd, and Texas Instruments.

TOM VAN STEENHOVEN is Business Storyteller, Starizon, Inc. After Tom's humble beginnings as an actor, musician, and director in live theater, he broke into advertising as a writer and has won every major national award for his work. He was Creative Director at his last two agencies for several national accounts. He discovered a love for film and has written and directed hundreds of TV spots, corporate videos, and short features. He became a freelance writer in the mid-1980s so that he could have time to pursue his own projects. Since then, he has written screenplays, children's books, novels, musical comedies, magazine articles, and music. For Starizon, Tom creates imaginative adventure stories, complete with maps and facilitator guidebooks, to help clients train their employees in an interactive, experiential way. He is the author of the original "Raiders of the Lost Art" employee engagement, and continues to create ongoing stories for all of Starizon's clients. To quote one of Tom's favorite phrases: "Storytelling reveals meaning without committing the error of defining it."